The
Sacrifice
Paradox

# The
# Sacrifice
# Paradox

## How To Navigate Life's Choices And Trade-Offs

## DAVID J. KALINOWSKI

INDIE BOOKS
INTERNATIONAL

# The Sacrifice Paradox

## How To Navigate Life's Choices And Trade-Offs

ISBN 13: 978-1-966168-46-1

Designed by: Melissa Farr, Back Porch Creative, LLC

INDIE BOOKS INTERNATIONAL®, INC.
2511 WOODLANDS WAY
OCEANSIDE, CA 92054
www.indiebooksintl.com

# Dedication

For every person who has stood at a crossroads,
uncertain which part of themselves to give up.

For those who've sacrificed, sometimes silently—
out of love, duty, or hope.

And for those still searching for that elusive balance
between holding on and letting go . . .
*This book is for you.*

# Contents

## Part II: 101 Inspiring Stories Of Sacrifices And Trade-Offs

## Part III: Reflection Guideposts

# Preface

Life is a series of calculated trade-offs. Some sacrifices fuel our greatest achievements, while others deplete us. The key isn't just making sacrifices—it's making *the right ones.*

The concept of sacrifice is not new; it has been an integral part of human history and culture for millennia. From ancient rituals where offerings were made to gods and deities, to the personal and professional sacrifices we make in our daily lives, the act of giving up something valuable is deeply ingrained in our existence. But what makes a sacrifice worthwhile? How do we know if the trade-off will lead to a better outcome?

In this book, we will delve into the complexities of sacrifices, examining the different forms they take and the impact they have on our lives. We will explore personal stories, insights from others, and practical guidance on how to navigate the complex terrain of sacrifices. My hope is that by the end of this journey, you will have a clearer understanding of how to make sacrifices that align with your values and lead to a more fulfilling life.

This book is for leaders, professionals, parents, caregivers, students, teachers, athletes, artists, entrepreneurs, and ambitious individuals who constantly navigate trade-offs in their careers and personal lives. If you've ever struggled with decisions about work-life balance, career moves, leadership responsibilities, or personal sacrifices, this book will help you make better, more strategic choices.

**David J. Kalinowski**
Chicago, Illinois

# PART I

# Success Is About Giving Up The Right Things

# 1 The Call That Changed Everything

’ll never forget the day my cell phone rang on my nightstand at 7 a.m. and woke me up. The date was Saturday, September 14, 2019. I thought about ignoring the call. You know the moment when you're half asleep, debating whether to answer. But something told me I should. So, with my eyes mostly closed, I picked up my phone and saw it was my mom.

"Hello?" I said groggily.

"David, David, David, something's wrong with your father," my mom said in a panic. "I'm at the hospital. I don't know what's wrong. They're saying he might not make it. I don't know what to do. I'm alone. I need help. What do I do?"

My mom's voice was trembling. I never heard her so emotional, and we're talking about a woman who is 100 percent Italian, so emotional days are common. But this? This was different.

My mind quickly started to process what was happening. I was a bit numb. At the same time, I selfishly had a flash of all the important plans I had scheduled that weekend, commitments made months in advance. I had a choice to make. I immediately decided to sacrifice those original weekend plans and get down to Florida.

I was out of bed, pacing.

"Mom, I need you to take a deep breath with me," I said calmly as I also took a breath. "Now take another. I'm getting dressed, heading straight to the airport, and will catch the first flight to Tampa. I need you to try to remain calm. I will be there as soon as I can, and we'll figure out together what's going on."

There was no question. No hesitation. Some sacrifices don't feel like choices at all.

### Reflection Questions

Think about a time when you had to make an urgent decision that disrupted your plans. How did you handle it? What did you learn from that experience?

# 2   Sacrifice Defined

S acrifice is one of those words that sounds heavy, like it belongs in an ancient ritual. But in reality? What is a sacrifice? I'm not talking about killing an animal in a religious ceremony as an offering to please a deity.

Sacrifices are an inevitable part of life. As author Stephen Covey put it: Sacrifice really means "giving up something good for something better."[1]

But how do we know which sacrifices will lead to something better?

Sometimes, what seems like a loss sets the stage for growth and greater opportunities. Other times, unnecessary sacrifices drain us and hold us back.

Let's explore what I call the Sacrifice Paradox. Sometimes, to gain something truly valuable, we must first give up something else that we also value. It's the notion that the very act of sacrifice, which seems like a loss, can lead to our greatest gains. It's a paradox because giving up something important might appear to be a setback, but it often leads to profound growth, success, and fulfillment.

## Lina's Career Selection

Lina had a promising career in finance, working long hours and climbing the corporate ladder. Lina was a rising executive in finance, advancing with relentless dedication. On paper, she was thriving. Inside, she felt empty. Since childhood, she had loved art. Painting was her passion, but she had convinced herself that a "real career" meant financial security.

She was on track for a senior executive position. However, her passion for art was something she had always pushed aside. One day, she made the terrifying decision to leave her six-figure job to pursue her dream of becoming a full-time artist.

The first few years were brutal—financial instability, self-doubt, constant struggle. But Lina kept going. Slowly, her work gained recognition. Commissions started rolling in. Today, Lina is a successful professional artist, known for her unique style and creativity, not only financially stable but personally fulfilled.

### Reflection Questions

Identify an area in your life where you might need to make a sacrifice to pursue a passion. What is the potential gain? What fears are holding you back?

# 3 Historical Context Of Sacrifice

Sacrifice has always been a part of human civilization. In ancient times, people made sacrifices to gods and deities, hoping to gain favor or avert disaster. These sacrifices often involved giving up something of great value, such as livestock, crops, or even human lives. The idea was that by giving up something valuable, individuals and communities could secure a better future.

While the nature of sacrifices has evolved over time, the underlying principle remains the same. Today, we may not offer livestock to appease gods, but we do make sacrifices in our personal and professional lives. We give up time, comfort, and resources to achieve our goals and support our loved ones.

We sacrifice time for financial security.
We sacrifice comfort for personal growth.
We sacrifice personal interests for
the well-being of our families.

The modern-day sacrifices we make may seem less dramatic than those of the past, but they are no less significant. The key is understanding which sacrifices serve us and which hold us back.

# 4 The Personal Impact Of Sacrifice

Sacrifices often require us to give up something that we hold dear. This can be incredibly challenging, as it forces us to confront our deepest desires and values. The act of sacrificing can lead to feelings of loss and regret, but it can also pave the way for growth and fulfillment.

Consider the parent who decides to stay at home to raise their children, sacrificing their career aspirations and financial stability. This decision is not made lightly, as it involves a trade-off between personal ambition and family responsibilities. However, the rewards of being present during the formative years of their children's lives can far outweigh the sacrifices made.

Similarly, think about the entrepreneur who gives up a stable job to pursue their dream of starting a business. The path is fraught with uncertainty and risk, but the potential for success and personal satisfaction drives them forward. These sacrifices are made in the hope of achieving something greater, something that aligns with their true purpose.

# 5 Professional Impact Of Sacrifice

I n the professional realm, sacrifices often involve giving up personal time and comfort to achieve career goals. This can mean working long hours, missing family events, and enduring significant stress. However, these sacrifices can lead to career advancement, financial rewards, and a sense of accomplishment. These sacrifices include:

- *Working long hours* at the expense of personal relationships
- *Relocating for a job opportunity* despite leaving friends and family behind
- *Taking on additional responsibilities* with no immediate financial gain

While these sacrifices may lead to career advancement and financial rewards, they can also result in burnout and lost personal connections. The challenge lies in finding a balance between professional aspirations and personal well-being.

It is easy to get caught up in the pursuit of success, neglecting the relationships and activities that bring joy and fulfillment. The key is to make conscious choices that align with your values and long-term goals.

### Reflection Question

Are you sacrificing in a way that aligns with your long-term values, or are you making short-term sacrifices that drain your energy without meaningful rewards?

# 6 Navigating The Sacrifice Paradox

The Sacrifice Paradox highlights the complexity of making sacrifices. It is not always clear whether a sacrifice will lead to the desired outcome, and the process often involves significant uncertainty and risk. However, by understanding your values and priorities, you can make informed decisions that align with your true purpose.

For years, we've been sold the idea that success comes from doing more: more work, more hustle, more commitments.

This is *the Sacrifice Paradox*: We believe that success requires more effort, but true success often requires strategic choices and intentional sacrifices.

What's the problem? Most of us are giving up the wrong things!

*What if the key to success isn't doing more, but sacrificing or giving up the right things?*

From my personal experiences and observing others, there are three types of sacrifices we seem to make, whether we realize it or not:

## Three Types Of Sacrifices

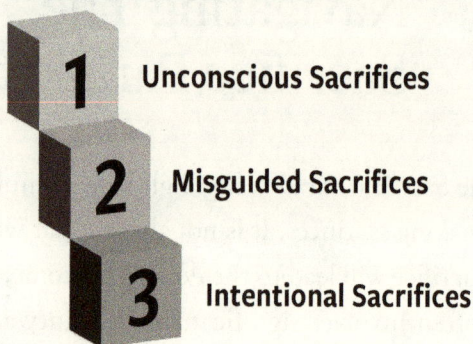

**1**   **Unconscious Sacrifices**

**2**   **Misguided Sacrifices**

**3**   **Intentional Sacrifices**

- *Unconscious sacrifices.* These are the hidden trade-offs that happen without deliberate choice. They creep into our lives through habit, routine, and external expectations. We sacrifice time with loved ones because work feels urgent. We sacrifice health by neglecting sleep, skipping meals, or living in constant stress. These sacrifices aren't intentional; they accumulate in the background until the cost becomes painfully clear. What is the harm? We often don't recognize them until it's too late.

- *Misguided sacrifices.* These are the sacrifices we *think* will lead to success, but work against us. Saying "yes" to every opportunity, stretching ourselves too thin, and mistaking busyness for productivity are common examples. We trade deep work for endless meetings, sacrifice personal fulfillment for professional status, and prioritize urgent tasks over important ones. The danger? We believe these sacrifices are necessary, but they drain us without meaningful returns. Even Harvard Business School Professor Michael Porter, a leading authority on competitive strategy, says strategy involves knowing what to say "no" to—well, so do the sacrifices we make.[2]

- *Intentional sacrifices.* These are the sacrifices that unlock true success. They are the conscious decisions to let go of what is merely good in favor of what is truly great. This means choosing deep focus over constant availability, quality over quantity, and long-term impact over short-term gratification. Intentional sacrifices involve the ability to choose what to let go of to create space for what truly matters—whether it's meaningful work, personal fulfillment, or relationships that nourish us. What is the key? These sacrifices are made *by design*, not *by default*.

Throughout this book, we will explore various aspects of sacrifices, from the small daily choices to the significant, life-changing decisions. We will look at the impact of sacrifices on our personal and professional lives and provide practical guidance on how to navigate these complex trade-offs.

# 7   The Marathon Project

Imagine staying awake for 108 hours. Yes, you read that right—108 hours straight—no sleep, no fun, no time with friends or family. I'll do the math for you: that's 4.5 days.

I did it. Just my computer and me, fueled by a ridiculous amount of caffeine. Thank goodness for NoDoz and energy drinks (since I don't drink coffee). At one point, I started naming the icons on my desktop because I was the only one awake to keep them company.

Why? A major client project. A huge deadline that could not be missed. You know what I'm talking about. I was determined to deliver, and I did. The client loved it. We even secured repeat business.

But at what personal cost?

By the end, I'm pretty sure I was seeing unicorns galloping across my keyboard. I'd become numb to everything else—my phone was full of unread messages, I couldn't remember the last actual conversation I'd had that wasn't about revisions, and when it was finally over, I didn't feel proud. I felt empty. Exhausted. Disconnected. And oddly, a little sad that I had pushed myself that far to prove a point.

Sacrifice? Absolutely.

The trade-off was between proving my professional commitment and preserving my physical and emotional well-being.

The benefit was delivering excellence and earning client trust.

But the consequence was realizing that I had placed external validation above my own limits, and that kind of pace, unchecked, isn't sustainable.

Was it worth it?

I think my sleep-deprived brain would say "yes—after a long nap." But my soul? It might say, "Next time, take more breaks and don't overcommit."

# 8 The Wedding

My daughter Miranda met the love of her life while attending Michigan State University (they met in, of all places, a calculus class) and got married in 2022 in Detroit. So, despite being super busy at work, I cleared my schedule for Thursday and Friday before the wedding and the Monday after, knowing the pile of work would build, not diminish.

Was it worth sacrificing three days of work? *You're damn right it was!* No-brainer.

---

**Reflection Questions**

Have you missed an important family event because you chose to do something else that you thought at the time was more important? Was it? Do you regret it? How did it affect your relationships?

---

# The Wedding

# 9 Emma's Breaking Point

Emma had always been known as "the smart one." Top of her class, full academic scholarship, and a reputation among faculty for being the go-to student for any ambitious project. So when she was invited to join a cutting-edge neuroscience research team in her final year, she didn't hesitate. It was the kind of opportunity that could fast-track her into a top-tier grad program or even a published journal article before graduation.

The work was exhilarating, but consuming.

Emma began living by lab schedules, not clocks. She skipped meals, turned down every social invite, and missed three family birthdays in a row. Her body started sending signals—insomnia and constant fatigue—but she brushed them off. *Just a few more weeks*, she told herself. *Then I'll rest.*

The *trade-off* was between immediate achievement and her long-term well-being.

The *benefit* was significant: glowing recommendations, publication credit, and a full ride to a prestigious graduate school.

But the *consequence* was hitting a wall, physically and emotionally. One morning, she fainted in the lab and was forced to take medical leave. It wasn't failure that stopped her. It was her own body waving the red flag she'd ignored for too long.

It took months for Emma to rebuild, not just her health, but her perspective. She didn't regret the project. But she did regret assuming that success had to come at the cost of herself.

Now, she treats her calendar differently. Lab time still matters, but so do sleep, friends, and boundaries. Balance isn't a luxury anymore. It's a requirement.

### Reflection Questions

Have you ever mistaken overachievement for resilience? What warning signs did you ignore—and what did you learn about your limits?

# 10 Michael's Orders

ichael had spent over two decades in the military, rising through the ranks with discipline, loyalty, and pride. He had led missions across continents, trained younger officers, and made personal sacrifices without hesitation. The uniform was more than a job; it was his identity.

But the deeper he rose, the more often home became a place he visited, not lived in.

When his daughter, Kayla, entered her senior year of high school, Michael promised himself he'd be there for the college visits, for the prom photos, for graduation. But just two weeks before her ceremony, a classified overseas assignment landed on his desk. It was one that would require immediate deployment. His commanding officer made it clear: "*You're the right person for this.*"

Michael had never said no to an order. But this time, he hesitated.

He sat with it for days, replaying Kayla's childhood milestones he had missed: her first recital, the fifth-grade science fair, her driver's test. He remembered the way she once said, "*It's okay, Dad, I'm used to it,*" as if that made it better.

This time, he said no.

The *trade-off* was between military responsibility and irreplaceable family connection.

The *benefit* was witnessing his daughter cross the stage, locking eyes with her as she beamed in cap and gown.

The *consequence* was internal, wrestling with guilt, explaining the preference to his commanding officer, and sitting with the uneasy feeling of placing family ahead of duty, just this once.

But the reward came weeks later, in a simple handwritten card: "*Thank you for choosing me, Dad. You have no idea what that meant.*"

### Reflection Questions

Have you ever had to disappoint one responsibility to honor another? How did you carry the weight of that decision—and what did it teach you about presence?

# 11    Everyday Dilemmas

**B**ut what about the gray zones? What about the sacrifices that are not as grand, make you hesitate, cause you to second-guess, aren't so clear-cut, and sometimes even cause you to regret your decision later?

When you are at a restaurant, and looking to eat healthier, do you choose that greasy, yet delicious, burger or a healthier salad? Well, how about the burger with no bun? That's healthier, right?

Do you work late or make it to your kid's band concert? Will they remember that you got the project done, or will they remember looking for you in the audience and not finding you?

Do you move for a promotion, uprooting your family? You get a bigger paycheck and a fancy title, but at what cost? Your kids are changing schools and leaving their friends behind, your spouse is finding a new job, and you're adjusting to a completely new life. Is it worth it?

Do I take my spouse out for dinner and miss my favorite sports team play?

Will I ever sacrifice time away from my family, again, working all night, to send my manager what they wanted to meet an urgent deadline, only to then get an automated out-of-office reply from them immediately after I hit "send"?

Do I miss the college toga party to study for my huge test? Hell no! I'm not missing that party. I'll still get a B on that test. I'd rather make memories with my friends.

Do I leave the workplace where I love what I do and enjoy the people I work with for more money elsewhere, with uncertain outcomes?

Do I fast for a day or two to jump-start my metabolism and optimize my weight loss program?

## What Choices Are You Making?

 or

# 12 Jessica's Predicament

J essica had been a nurse for over twelve years. She loved her patients, her coworkers, and the satisfaction of making a difference during people's hardest moments. But the long shifts, rotating holidays, and constant emotional weight had begun to blur the boundaries between work and life.

Her daughter, Ava, had been preparing for her first piano recital for months. She practiced in the early mornings before school and every evening after dinner, often asking, "*Will you be there in the front row, Mom?*"

Jessica's heart sank when she saw the posted shift. She was scheduled for that night. She considered asking for coverage, but it was flu season, and the floor was already short-staffed. Swapping shifts would mean asking someone else to work a double.

She agonized for days. She had never been the nurse who left a team hanging. But she also knew that Ava wouldn't have a "do-over" for this moment.

After a conversation with a colleague and a carefully crafted schedule change, Jessica made it to the recital—front row, smiling, teary-eyed, and clapping louder than anyone in the auditorium.

The *trade-off* was between professional loyalty and showing up for a once-in-a-lifetime moment.

The *benefit* was a memory etched in both her and Ava's hearts forever.

The *consequence* was the guilt she carried for shifting the burden to a teammate—and the clarity it gave her about what kind of balance she needed to reclaim in her life.

Later, she told her supervisor, *"I'm still committed to this job. But I also want to stay committed to the little girl who only gets one childhood."*

### Reflection Questions

When have you felt torn between your personal life and your responsibilities to others? What did you choose—and why?

# 13 Baseball And Chess

Think about a baseball player who hits a sacrifice fly. They step up to the plate, knowing the goal isn't personal glory or boosting their batting average. They swing not to get on base, but to hit the ball high and deep, just far enough to give the runner on third base a chance to tag up and score.

· From a statistical standpoint, the player records an out. It won't show up as a hit. It may even slightly dent their batting average. But in terms of the team? It's a success. One run closer to winning the game.

It's a subtle yet powerful moment in baseball, a selfless act in a sport where individual stats often dominate headlines. It says: *"I'm willing to give up my chance to shine if it moves the team forward."*

Now consider a very different arena: the chessboard.

Imagine a player choosing to sacrifice a valuable piece—say, a rook—not out of desperation, but with foresight.

They make the move knowing it will lure their opponent into a false sense of advantage. That calculated loss sets up a strategy that allows them to capture the queen a few turns later.

In chess, as in life, the best moves are not always the most obvious ones. Sometimes you give something up not out of defeat, but because you're playing a longer game. You're thinking a few moves ahead.

Both examples, though from very different worlds, offer the same lesson: sometimes sacrifice isn't about loss. It's about leverage. It's about letting go of something now to gain something more important later.

A statistic. A piece. A moment of credit. Even a dream.

In sports, in strategy, in life, we all face situations where we must decide: *Am I willing to take the out to get the run? Am I willing to let go of something valuable to move closer to what really matters?*

# 14 The Entrepreneur's Leap

Alex had a stable job with a reliable paycheck and predictable hours. It wasn't thrilling, but it offered security. But a dream had been growing inside him for years. The dream of starting his own business. He spent evenings sketching ideas, running numbers, and researching the market, always waiting for the "right time."

Eventually, he realized that waiting any longer might mean never trying at all. So, with a mix of excitement and fear, Alex resigned from his job and went all in on his entrepreneurial vision.

The first few years were brutal. Income was inconsistent. He downsized his apartment, sold his car, and passed on vacations and social outings. There were weeks when he questioned everything, especially during moments when bills piled up and nothing seemed to go right.

But Alex kept pushing forward. He adapted. He learned. He leaned on his vision when motivation was low. Slowly, things began to turn. Clients came, referrals followed, and the business started to grow. Over time, his company not only became profitable but also gave him the autonomy and fulfillment he had always wanted.

The *trade-off* was clear: immediate comfort for long-term possibility.

The *benefit* was building something of his own and proving to himself that the risk was worth it.

The *consequence* was a difficult stretch that tested his confidence and finances, but it also shaped his character and resilience in ways no corporate job ever could.

Alex's story reminds us that sacrifice is often the price of chasing something more meaningful.

### Reflection Questions

Think of a time when you made a strategic sacrifice. What was the outcome? Did it lead to the desired result you hoped for, or something unexpectedly better?

# 15 The Stay-At-Home Parent

Not all sacrifices come with ceremony or applause. Some happen in the space between a resignation letter and a whisper of a baby monitor.

Jordan had built a promising career in finance. The hours were long, but the pay was good and the promotions steady. When their second child was born, Jordan and their partner sat down with spreadsheets and calendars to figure out how to make life work. Childcare costs were high, and the idea of rushing home every night just to catch the last five minutes before bedtime felt wrong.

So Jordan stepped back. Not because it made sense on paper, but because it felt right in their heart.

The transition wasn't easy. Gone were the structured days, the sense of accomplishment from a closed deal, the adult conversation. Instead came diapers, dishes, storytime, and long afternoons that blurred into early evenings. There was no performance review to confirm they were doing it right.

The *trade-off* was that career momentum, financial growth, and professional identity were exchanged for a season of full-time parenting.

The *benefit* was life-changing: being present for first steps, tearful tantrums, giggles at snack time, and bedtime rituals that became cherished routines.

The *consequence* was a loss of professional visibility and the occasional sense of doubt. But the richness of presence made space for a new kind of fulfillment that no title or paycheck could replicate.

It wasn't a pause in Jordan's life. It was a redefinition of what progress looked like.

### Reflection Question

How do you determine the value of intangible rewards—like presence and connection—when weighing them against measurable gains like income or status?

# 16 The Teacher's Fulfillment

Linda was a teacher who truly loved her job. However, when her son was diagnosed with a developmental disorder, she decided to take a break from her career to care for him full-time.

The decision was challenging, as it meant giving up her professional aspirations and financial stability. But Linda's sacrifice allowed her to provide the support her son needed.

Over time, she found fulfillment in seeing her son's progress and knowing that her presence made a significant difference in his life.

### Reflection Questions

Have you ever made a sacrifice for a family member? What impact did it have on both of your lives?

# 17 The Soldier's Responsibility

Samuel had been in the military for over a decade. He was known for his discipline, his confidence, and his unwavering sense of duty. He had missed anniversaries, birthdays, and his son's first steps—not because he didn't care, but because he had made peace with the sacrifices his uniform required.

When a high-risk overseas mission was announced, Samuel was one of the first to volunteer. His wife didn't try to stop him. She simply asked, *"Are you sure this is the right time?"* Their son had just started middle school and was struggling to adjust. His daughter had been having nightmares about him not coming home.

But Samuel felt the weight of his calling. He had trained for this. He knew the mission mattered. And in his heart, he believed that protecting the lives of many sometimes came at the cost of being present for a few.

The *trade-off* was between being there for his family and stepping into a role that demanded complete commitment.

The *benefit* was fulfilling a purpose he had sworn to uphold, defending others, leading his team, and serving a cause bigger than himself.

The *consequence* was deep and lasting. He returned home a hero, but also a stranger. His children had grown. His absence had left gaps that no medal could fill.

Samuel didn't regret the mission, but he carried its price in more than memory. He carried it in the relationships that changed while he was gone.

### Reflection Questions

Have you ever chosen purpose or duty over personal connection? What did that decision cost—and what did it teach you about loyalty?

# 18 The Firefighter's Heroism

J oe had been a firefighter for nearly twenty years. He loved the camaraderie, the sense of purpose, and the adrenaline rush of responding to a call. But what he valued most was the knowledge that his work made a difference—that when people were at their most vulnerable, he could be the one running in when everyone else was running out.

One frigid January night, a call came in about a house engulfed in flames. By the time Joe's team arrived, the fire had spread to the upper floors. A neighbor shouted that a young child was still inside, trapped in a second-story bedroom.

Joe didn't hesitate. He located a possible entry point and charged in with zero visibility and only instinct to guide him. The heat was intense. The floorboards groaned. He found the child curled in a corner, unconscious from smoke inhalation. Cradling the child in one arm, he radioed for backup and made his way back, just moments before part of the ceiling collapsed behind him.

The child survived. So did Joe, but not without consequence.

The *trade-off* was between personal safety and the life of another.

The *benefit* was saving a child's life and honoring the promise of his calling.

The *consequence* was severe: Joe suffered third-degree burns and nerve damage that ended his career. He missed a year of his life in recovery and struggled with the transition from being the rescuer to needing support himself.

Joe doesn't tell the story to be called a hero. He tells it to remind people that courage isn't the absence of fear. It's the resolve to move through it when someone else needs you most.

### Reflection Questions

Have you ever seen someone put themselves at risk for the sake of others? What stayed with you about that moment—and how has it shaped your view of courage?

# 19 The Sacrifice Framework

S o, to help with this struggle on how to navigate these decisions, I developed the Sacrifice Framework, a sacrifice reasoning strategy for you to consider, helping better balance short-term, more emotional drivers with a long-term perspective.

In life, you have emotion on one end of the line and logic on the other, and in the middle is common sense. But because short-term thinking is often associated with emotions, we need a framework or strategy to be sure we remind ourselves that emotions are not the only voice.

## The Sacrifice Framework
Sacrifices are rarely black and white—but the tough choices we face often have clearer implications than we realize.

This framework helps you assess whether a sacrifice is worth making by examining two key dimensions:

1. *Impact on Self*

2. *Impact on Others*

See a simple 2x2 grid. Each quadrant represents a different type of sacrifice decision:

- *Top Right: Sacrifice*

  These are the moments when your sacrifice benefits both you and others. It might require effort or discomfort, but it aligns with your values and creates mutual gain. These are the "green light" sacrifices.

- *Bottom Left: Don't Sacrifice*

  These choices help no one—not you, and not others. They deplete your time, energy, or identity without a meaningful return. These are the sacrifices we must learn to say no to.

- *Top Left: Maybe Sacrifice*

  Here, the sacrifice benefits you but not others. It might feel necessary in the short term—like leaving a team to pursue a personal goal—but it's worth weighing the relational or ethical cost.

- *Bottom Right: Maybe Sacrifice*

  In this quadrant, your sacrifice helps others but not yourself. These choices can feel noble, but over time, they may lead to burnout or resentment. Ask yourself: *Is it sustainable? Is it being recognized?*

When viewed in grayscale, this framework is not about color—it's about clarity. It's about learning to pause, reflect, and ask not just "*Can I give this up?*" but "*Should I?*"

By using this framework, you can ensure that *every sacrifice is intentional, sustainable, and aligned with your values.*

## SACRIFICE FRAMEWORK

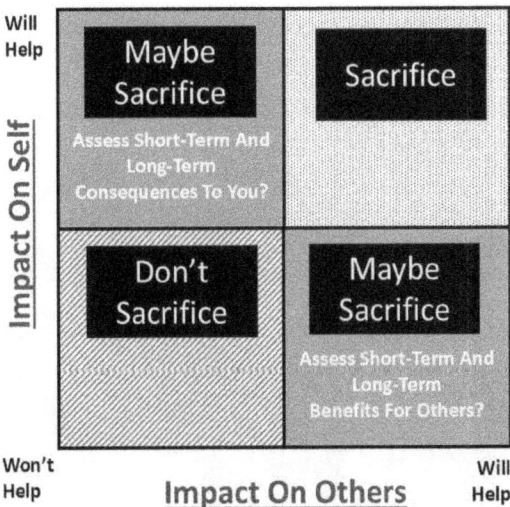

When assessing the benefits or consequences of the sacrifices, fall back on your purpose.

# 20 Leadership And Corporate Culture

L eadership is about setting the *cultural tone* for how sacrifices are made and managed within an organization. Every company demands trade-offs— whether it's an executive deciding to forgo short-term profits for long-term growth, or an employee choosing between personal time and meeting a deadline.

The best leaders understand that sacrifices must be mutual and strategic, not forced upon employees without consideration. When employees see leadership making fair, values-driven sacrifices, they are more likely to engage, remain loyal, and trust the company's vision.

In business, leadership is about making strategic choices and intentional sacrifices. Successful leaders understand that short-term discomfort is often necessary for long-term gain. Leaders set the tone for how sacrifice is viewed and managed within an organization. The culture they create affects how employees perceive work-life balance, personal commitments, and long-term career choices.

Some organizations foster a healthy culture of sacrifice, where employees are willing to make trade-offs because they see a clear purpose and benefit. Others create a toxic environment, where sacrifices feel like demands rather than choices.

This section explores how leaders navigate corporate trade-offs—balancing financial constraints, employee well-being, and organizational growth—and how their decisions shape workplace culture.

## The Role Of Leadership In Workplace Sacrifices

Every organization requires sacrifice at some level. Employees work long hours, take on extra projects, and sometimes put personal life on hold for professional growth.

- But when does sacrifice become too much?
- How can leaders ensure sacrifices are meaningful rather than draining?
- Effective leaders understand that balancing individual and organizational needs is crucial. Employees will go the extra mile when they feel valued, respected, and fairly compensated for their contributions.

## Common Workplace Trade-offs

- Work-life balance versus career advancement: Should an employee miss family events to meet tight deadlines?
- Long-term innovation versus short-term profits: Should a company invest in research and development at the cost of immediate financial performance?
- Employee well-being versus productivity goals: Should leadership push teams harder, or focus on sustainable success?

Poor leadership forces employees into constant, unacknowledged sacrifices, leading to burnout and disengagement. Strong leadership ensures that sacrifices feel purposeful and that employees see a clear connection between their efforts and long-term rewards.

## Sacrificing Short-Term Gains For Long-Term Success

Great leaders delay gratification for greater future rewards. Companies that thrive often make strategic sacrifices today to secure lasting success.

### Example: Amazon's Long-Term Investment Strategy

Amazon operated at a financial loss for years, reinvesting in infrastructure, technology, and customer experience rather than seeking immediate profitability. This decision positioned Amazon as a dominant force in e-commerce.

## Example: Leaders Taking Pay Cuts Instead Of Layoffs

During economic downturns, some leaders, including myself, take voluntary salary cuts to retain employees rather than enforcing mass layoffs. This approach fosters employee trust, loyalty, and long-term productivity. Leaders who make personal sacrifices alongside their employees inspire stronger commitment and deeper engagement.

## Creating A Sustainable Culture Of Sacrifice

For sacrifices to be meaningful and effective, they must be:

- Intentional: Employees must understand the purpose behind their efforts.
- Recognized: Contributions should be acknowledged and rewarded.
- Sustainable: Sacrifices should not lead to burnout or resentment.

If employees feel sacrifices are expected but not appreciated, they will become disengaged. On the other hand, when they see a shared vision, personal growth opportunities, and fair compensation, they willingly commit to the organization's success.

## Leadership Strategies For Healthy Sacrifice

The following are strategies that leaders employ for healthy sacrifices:

- Transparency in decision-making: Explain why trade-offs are necessary.
- Provide support systems: Offer professional development and wellness programs.
- Encourage balance: Recognize employees' personal lives and time commitments.
- Leaders don't just ask for sacrifices—they make sacrifices themselves to build a thriving, purpose-driven company culture.

## Case Study: Leadership During A Crisis

A small business owner faced a financial downturn where *mass layoffs* seemed inevitable. Instead of cutting jobs, she did the following:

- Eliminated executive bonuses
- Implemented temporary 20–40 percent salary reductions for top earners
- Paused unnecessary expenditures to preserve cash

By taking these steps, she was able to accomplish the following:

- Preserve employee morale
- Retain top talent
- Strengthen long-term company culture

Her leadership ensured that sacrifices were fair, transparent, and aligned with the organization's values.

In my experience, having worked with over 225 Fortune 1000 organizations, I have seen effective leaders understand that balancing individual and organizational needs is crucial. And I've seen leaders who just don't get it.

Poor leadership forces employees into constant, unacknowledged sacrifices, leading to burnout and disengagement. And guess what, burnout tends to happen when sacrifice is for everyone but you!

## Leadership As The Model For Sacrifice

- The best leaders don't just demand sacrifices from their teams—they lead by example.
- They create environments where sacrifices feel worthwhile, where the long-term mission is clear, and where employees feel valued and respected.
- When leadership aligns sacrifice with purpose, it transforms from an obligation into an opportunity for shared growth and success.

### Reflection Questions
Think of a situation where you had to make a difficult decision that affected others. How did you handle it? What was the outcome?

Culture determines whether sacrifices are seen as investments in a shared mission or as imposed burdens. In toxic workplaces, employees feel forced to sacrifice, leading to resentment. In healthy workplaces, sacrifices feel purposeful—as part of a collective effort.

One clothing company is known for its employee-centric policies, proving that a strong culture reduces employee turnover and enhances productivity. They offer the following:

- On-site childcare to ease work-family trade-offs
- Paid time off for activism, aligning with company values
- A results-driven culture, rather than a "face-time" requirement

This mutual approach to sacrifice ensures that employees remain engaged and willing to make trade-offs when necessary.

# 21  Survey Results

I was curious about what others thought about this sacrifice topic and how it resonated with them.

I ran an online survey to get directional input on this topic. I received 134 responses. So, while one can debate if this is a statistically valid sample size, at a minimum, the results provided some interesting directional information.

About 96 percent of responses came from baby boomers, Gen X, and millennials. When asked if they were willing to sacrifice something family-related for work, 76 percent across all generations said "yes." When asked if they were willing to sacrifice something work-related for family, the percentage across all generations shot up to 92 percent.

How do we know if we should make a sacrifice? Mostly, when faced with the need to make a sacrifice, we rely on our past judgment. What did we learn from the last time? Sometimes we didn't learn anything because we repeated the same mistake or choice that may have been okay short-term, but was hurtful long-term.

But how do people decide if they should make the sacrifice? When I posed that question, the top three factors considered were:

1. The impact it would have on family (note the impact could be positive or negative).
2. The sacrifice was being made only because one felt a sense of obligation.
3. There would be professional growth.

I do want to pause and share that if you are making a sacrifice because you feel obligated, be cautious before making your decision. You may feel obligated to leave work earlier than you desire because a spouse or child makes you feel guilty; you may feel obligated to stay longer on the project because you think, "After all, my boss and the team count on me to finish the job," even if it's their responsibility.

From my life experiences, in observing others and getting feedback from people, making a sacrifice repeatedly because you feel obligated often leads to resentment, which I'll address a little later. So, if the only reason you are making the sacrifice is because of a sense of obligation, it warrants more conversation with the parties involved before you choose to make that sacrifice.

When asked if the respondents think more about short-term or long-term impact at the time of the sacrifice, nearly 70 percent stated they think mostly about the short-term impact. And that's part of our problem!

Author and journalist, Suzy Welch (who, yes, has a husband named Jack Welch), in her 2009 book *10-10-10* describes a rule for tough decisions:[3]

1. How will you feel about your decision ten minutes from now?
2. How about ten months from now?
3. How about ten years from now?

She talks about when making a short-term decision, the feeling now is intense and sharp, while the future feels fuzzier, and this gives the present too much power and by applying this 10-10-10 rule, it helps to shift our spotlight and to imagine a moment in the future with the same freshness that we feel in the present.

There was an employee at my firm, Proactive Worldwide, who came to me one day—completely out of the blue—and said they needed a $10,000 raise. I reminded them that they had recently received a generous salary increase based on their role and performance. Yet, they insisted. So, I asked a simple question: "What additional value do you expect to provide in return for this increase?"

Their response? "None."

They explained that they had received an offer from another company for $10,000 more and would be leaving unless I matched it.

I genuinely valued this team member's contributions. But they were already at the upper end of our salary band for that role. I encouraged them to take a step back and evaluate the full compensation package—not just the base salary. They were laser-focused on the paycheck. So I asked them to also consider whether the new company's culture aligned with what they truly wanted in a workplace.

They chose to leave.

About four months later, they reached out indirectly by contacting a former colleague who currently worked with us. That colleague passed along a message: They admitted they had made a mistake.

What had they discovered? Their new company offered only two weeks of vacation, compared to the four weeks they had with us. They now received just five paid holidays, whereas we had offered eleven, plus two floating holidays and even their birthday off with pay. They also learned, a bit too late, that while Proactive shuts down for the last two weeks of the year—paid time off specifically for rest and recharge, they now had no such benefit. All told, they had sacrificed five to six weeks of time off for a $10,000 raise, which translated to about $625 more per month after taxes.

As it turned out, they and their spouse were expecting a new baby. They expressed that additional time off would have been incredibly valuable.

They also shared that they didn't like their new manager, felt disconnected from their teammates, and were struggling in a cutthroat culture that didn't reflect their values. None of those factors had been carefully considered when they made their emotionally driven decision to leave.

This is exactly why I talk about the Sacrifice Framework. It exists to prompt people to pause and reflect—not just on the short-term, emotional appeal of a choice and trade-off, but on the long-term benefits and consequences. A raise may look appealing on paper, but what you gain in dollars may cost you in peace, time, and alignment.

# 22 Jane's Unfinished Launch

J ane was a rising star in her company's marketing department—driven, strategic, and trusted to lead the firm's biggest product rollout in over a decade. She'd spent months preparing: late nights, meticulous planning, and cross-functional meetings stacked back-to-back. She was determined to make it a career-defining moment.

Then, the news that changed everything. Her mother had been diagnosed with early-stage dementia. Though not a medical emergency, it meant a series of appointments, tough decisions, and an urgent need for emotional presence.

Jane didn't leave right away. At first, she tried to juggle both—taking calls from hospital waiting rooms and editing launch copy between check-ins. But the cracks started to show. Her work quality dipped, her temper shortened, and guilt crept in from both sides.

Eventually, Jane made a difficult decision: she stepped away from the project before launch. She passed the baton to a colleague she trusted, knowing she wouldn't be the one in the press release or on stage.

The *trade-off* was between professional visibility and being fully present for someone who had once rearranged her whole world for Jane.

The *benefit* was deeper than recognition—it was reconnection. Jane spent those weeks with her mother capturing memories, organizing care, and laughing about old stories.

The *consequence* was emotional more than practical. She wrestled with feelings of professional invisibility and fear of falling behind. But in time, she realized she hadn't stepped back—she'd simply stepped into something more important.

### Reflection Questions

Have you ever chosen to step away from the spotlight to support someone behind the scenes? What did that moment teach you about what truly matters?

# 23 More Everyday Trade-Offs

**B**elow are several common trade-offs we may face in our everyday lives.

## The Fitness Trade-Off

How many of us have skipped a workout because of a busy schedule or to binge-watch our favorite show like *Yellowstone, Suits, Big Brother, Survivor,* or *The Bachelorette*? And yes, I watch *The Bachelor* and *The Bachelorette*. Don't judge me. The trade-off is immediate comfort versus long-term health.

It could be the other way, too, where you skip watching TV to get your workout in. Or, some wake up early to get a workout in before other commitments, sacrificing sleep.

## Career Advancement Versus Personal Time

A promotion might mean uprooting your life to move to a new city. The job promises career growth and a higher salary, but it means the kids have to change schools and leave behind friends, family, and the life they've built. The sacrifice is not just about changing jobs; it's about uprooting your entire life for potential professional gain. Is it worth it?

One friend told me that when he sacrifices time from his family to engage in work, he is doing it for his family. His wife didn't see it that way and would often complain about all his work hours, so he said, "Fine, I can go get a job tomorrow and be home daily by 5 p.m., but I will be making $40,000 a year—and we will need to downsize our house, take the kids out of private school, stop eating out so often, eliminate exotic trips, cancel all nail and spa treatments, I will have to give up golf, and we'll have to massively cut back on saving for our retirement." And if you can believe it, she never let his work bother her again. She accepted the trade-off.

## Social Events Versus Personal Rest

How often do you choose between attending a friend's Friday night social event and needing personal rest? The sacrifice here involves balancing the need to maintain social connections with your own health and well-being.

Apply the Sacrifice Framework to these kinds of situations in your life to help inform your decision.

# 24 Sam's Start-Up

S am was fiercely ambitious about launching his own tech company. He'd spent years dreaming of building something from scratch, something disruptive, scalable, and uniquely his. But he knew the price of that dream would be steep: long nights, relentless pressure, financial uncertainty, and a dramatically reduced social life.

He pushed forward anyway.

Sam poured his life savings into the venture, skipped vacations, and barely saw his closest friends. When a key investor meeting was scheduled for the same weekend as his best friend's wedding, he chose the pitch. "Just this once," he told himself. "They'll understand." The company eventually secured the deal, but the friendship never fully recovered.

The *trade-off* was clear: Sam sacrificed personal milestones and relationships in pursuit of professional success.

The *benefit* was undeniable: his company grew, his reputation soared, and he experienced the thrill of building something meaningful from the ground up.

The *consequence*, however, lingered: missed moments he couldn't get back, friends who drifted away, and a sense of disconnection that even success couldn't fully fill.

In time, Sam came to realize that ambition and balance don't have to be mutually exclusive. The startup taught him about innovation, but the sacrifice taught him about value.

### Reflection Questions

Think of a recent trade-off you made. How did it affect your life? Was it worth it? How did it make you feel? How did it make others feel?

# 25 Lisa's Volunteer Work

L isa was a successful lawyer who genuinely enjoyed her work. She thrived in high-stakes negotiations, earned the respect of her peers, and had built a career she was proud of. But as the years passed, Lisa began to feel an emptiness she couldn't ignore—a tug to serve her community in a more personal, human way.

Answering that call, she began volunteering at a local women's shelter on weekends. She helped with legal advocacy, coached residents on interview prep, and often just listened—truly listened—to people who felt invisible in the world.

The *trade-off* was that Lisa sacrificed her leisure time, gave up restful weekends, and occasionally had to rearrange professional obligations to accommodate her volunteer work.

The *benefit* was that her time at the shelter brought her a deep sense of purpose and connection that no courtroom victory ever could. She rediscovered parts of herself she had long buried beneath deadlines and billable hours.

The *consequence* was that Lisa often felt stretched thin. Her social life took a hit, and she sometimes faced skepticism from colleagues who didn't understand why she was "giving so much away." There were moments of exhaustion, missed networking opportunities, and doubts.

But she never regretted it. In serving others, Lisa found a deeper version of success. One built not just on achievement, but on alignment with her values.

### Reflection Questions

Reflect on a time when you volunteered or helped someone in need. How did it make you feel? What did you learn from the experience?

# 26 Rachel's Journey

**R**achel was a high-powered executive in a multinational company. She loved her job but felt something was missing. She decided to take a sabbatical to travel and volunteer in different countries. This meant sacrificing her career progression and financial stability.

Rachel's journey was transformative. She discovered new cultures, met incredible people, and found a deeper sense of purpose. When she returned, she had a renewed perspective on life and work. The sacrifice was worth it, as it brought her fulfillment and clarity.

### Reflection Questions

When is the last time you took time to truly think and seek clarity? Have you made the necessary changes in life to gain personal fulfillment?

# 27 Tom's Passion Project

Tom was a successful software engineer who always dreamed of writing a novel. For years, he juggled his demanding job with late-night writing sessions, sacrificing sleep and social activities.

After dozens of rejections, his book was published and became a bestseller. The joy and fulfillment Tom felt from achieving his dream outweighed the sacrifices he had made along the way. His story illustrates that persistence and passion can lead to extraordinary results.

**Reflection Questions**

Think about a significant sacrifice you made in the past. Did it pay off? How did it shape your life?

# 28 Align Sacrifice With Purpose

Does a sacrifice pay off? Sometimes yes, and sometimes no. I believe that sacrifices should align with your purpose.

My friend Matthew Kelly, bestselling author of dozens of books, stated in his 2004 book *The Rhythm of Life* that, "God wants us to become the best-version-of-yourself"[4] (a phrase you hear so many utter now) and that is our purpose. Simon Sinek speaks about "seeking fulfillment versus happiness."[5]

My personal purpose in life is "To make a positive difference in the lives of others."

## Sacrifices Should Align With Your Purpose

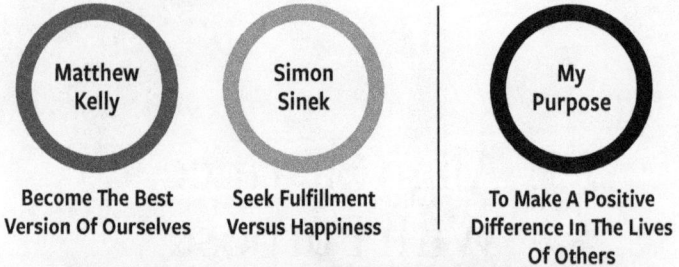

**Matthew Kelly**

**Simon Sinek**

**My Purpose**

**Become The Best Version Of Ourselves**

**Seek Fulfillment Versus Happiness**

**To Make A Positive Difference In The Lives Of Others**

Your Purpose And What You Sacrifice May Change As Life Evolves

Take some time to reflect on your true purpose.

A sacrifice *without* purpose becomes regret. A sacrifice *with* purpose becomes legacy and helps shape the story you leave behind.

Pause before deciding to make a sacrifice and apply the Sacrifice Framework. Talk with those in your professional and personal life about what trade-offs you will or will not make.

At the end of your life, it won't be the emails you sent, the deals you helped close, or the sleepless nights that define you.

To make better choices when faced with sacrifices, take the following steps:

1. Clarify your purpose and values. Understand what truly matters to you. Is it family, career, personal growth, or something else? Knowing your values will guide your decisions and priorities, and those priorities will change as you age.
2. Evaluate the long-term impact. Will the sacrifices lead to a fulfilling life, or will they cause regret?
3. Seek balance. Strive for a balance between personal and professional commitments. It's not always about choosing one over the other but finding a harmony that works for you.
4. Communicate. Talk to those affected by your choices. Their perspectives can help you make informed decisions.

Sometimes sacrifices lead to resentment toward oneself or others affected by the decision. This resentment often stems from a lack of communication, where the rationale behind the sacrifice remains unclear or misunderstood. When people do not understand why a choice was made, they fill in the gaps with their own assumptions—often leaning toward negative interpretations. This can breed frustration, misalignment, and emotional distance.

Consider a leader who chooses to cut a department's budget to allocate resources elsewhere. If employees only see the cut but never hear the reasoning, they may assume it was arbitrary or a sign that their work is undervalued.

Resentment grows because they feel unseen, unheard, and unappreciated.

However, if that same leader communicates the decision transparently, explaining the broader strategy and acknowledging the challenges, then although employees may disagree, they will at least understand the reasoning. This understanding diffuses much of the resentment that stems from feeling left in the dark.

The same dynamic plays out in personal relationships. Imagine a parent who works late hours to provide financial stability but never discusses the reason with their family. The spouse and children might interpret the absence as neglect or misplaced priorities, leading to bitterness. But if the parent openly explains the sacrifice and reassures their loved ones that they remain a priority, the emotional response shifts from resentment to appreciation, even if the hardship remains.

At its core, clear communication about sacrifice does not guarantee agreement, but it does foster understanding. When people understand the *why* behind a difficult choice, they may still feel the effects of the trade-off, but they are far less likely to hold onto anger or resentment. They can frame the situation with context rather than assumptions. This principle applies across all areas of life, from professional decision-making to personal sacrifices, reinforcing that open dialogue is the best antidote to resentment.

# 29 Mark's Family Decision

Mark was a project manager at a leading firm. He was offered a promotion that required relocating to another city. This move would benefit his career but would disrupt his family's life.

Mark discussed the opportunity with his wife and children, considering their perspectives. They decided to make the move together, understanding the challenges and benefits.

The transition was tough, but the family grew closer, supporting each other through the change. Mark's story underscores the importance of communication and mutual understanding in making sacrifices.

### Reflection Questions

When making a decision that affects family members, do you discuss it with them? How much do you truly weigh their considerations and the sacrifices they also would need to make from your decision?

# 30 Anna's Health Journey

Anna was a dedicated nurse who loved her job but often neglected her own health. After a health scare, she realized she needed to make significant lifestyle changes.

She started exercising regularly, eating healthier, and ensuring she got enough rest. This meant cutting back on overtime and declining some social invitations.

While it was challenging and required Anna to communicate what she was going through with her friends and coworkers, so they had a better understanding of her intentions, Anna's improved health and well-being were worth the sacrifices.

Her story highlights the importance of prioritizing self-care to lead a balanced and fulfilling life.

**Reflection Questions**

Think of a time when you had to communicate a difficult decision. How did you handle it? What was the outcome?

# 31 Ethan's Crossroads

**E**than was a gifted musician known for his soulful songwriting and raw, acoustic style. After years of small gigs and self-produced extended plays (EPs), a major record label finally offered him a contract. It was everything he thought he wanted: money, distribution, tour support—his name in lights.

But there was a catch.

The label wanted to reshape his image: autotuned pop tracks, co-written songs tailored for radio, and a heavily curated social media presence. "We'll make you famous," they said. "But you've got to play the game."

Ethan was torn. This was the opportunity every artist dreams about, but it meant abandoning the sound that made him fall in love with music in the first place. He pictured sold-out arenas and chart-topping hits, and also the peace of his bedroom, where his songs were honest and his.

After a week of agonizing indecision, Ethan turned the deal down.

The *trade-off* was between fast-track fame and staying true to his creative identity.

The *benefit* was preserving the integrity of his music and connecting with fans who valued authenticity.

The *consequence* was the uphill road—longer hours, smaller venues, and years of proving himself without industry backing.

Still, Ethan built a devoted following and eventually launched his own indie label. He didn't become a global sensation, but he became something better: a musician who never lost his voice.

### Reflection Questions

Have you ever been offered something that looked like success—but didn't feel like it? What did choosing authenticity over acceptance teach you?

# 32 My Final Decision

Life is a series of trade-offs. Some are easy. Some are gut-wrenching. Success isn't about how much you've added, it's about what you've been willing to let go of.

When I went to be with my mom in Florida that day in September 2019, the doctors told us my dad had a severe infection, and his condition was rapidly deteriorating. My eighty-eight-year-old dad, a United States Marine, needed hospice care.

And then—another choice.

It was now September 18, four days after I arrived. I had a workshop the next day in Chicago. Over fifty people had paid to be there. Many had flown in already. It was my content. No one else could deliver it. What should I do?

I faced a difficult dilemma: staying with my fragile mom and sick, unconscious dad, or heading back home to Chicago to fulfill my professional responsibility to lead the workshop the next day.

I turned to my mom to discuss it. Without hesitation, she said, "Go; your work affects others and they're counting on you. It's what your father would want." Knowing my brother John was on his way down to be with her, soon followed by my brother Alan, added some comfort to my decision to leave, as I knew my mom would not be alone.

While this decision was emotionally challenging, it aligned with my values and purpose. It allowed me to fulfill my professional responsibilities and help others, and my mom's reassuring words eased some of the burden and guilt I felt.

Did I make the right sacrifice? I wrestled with that for months.

Sometimes, we don't regret what we sacrifice. We regret not communicating why. Sacrifices, when misunderstood, can lead to resentment. The best way to mitigate this? Communication.

Had I not discussed this with my mom, she might have resented me forever. Instead, my mom's words gave me peace: *"You were here when I needed you most."*

Days later, I got the call about midnight from the hospice nurse, and then my mom. I sat up in my bed, unable to speak. My father had passed away.

Shortly thereafter, my mom flew to Chicago to live with me, as it had been the plan for both parents to relocate before my dad got sick. She stayed with me for over two years, and I also had support from my brothers. My brother, Ed, would often come to get her so she could also stay near him every few weeks, and then he and my sister-in-law, Margo, took Mom in for a couple of years and cared for her.

Currently, at ninety years young, my mom resides with me and my wife Jennifer, and we love having her with us. It's time together we truly treasure. My brothers John and Alan continue to provide as much support as possible, and we're all doing our best to bring her happiness into her life. It's clear how deeply she misses my dad, especially after sixty-two years of marriage. I can only imagine the number of sacrifices they both made.

I'm deeply grateful for the ongoing support Ed and Margo provide. For many years, they cared for my mom and dad when they all lived in Florida, making their own sacrifices along the way, and today they continue to look after my mom, often welcoming her into their home.

As I reflect on this journey, I'm reminded that the greatest sacrifices are often made without recognition or applause, through small, everyday decisions that shape the lives of those we love. My parents modeled that for us, not just in grand gestures, but in daily acts of loyalty, patience, and devotion.

Now, as I care for my mother in her later years, I realize I'm walking a path they once walked for me. The roles reverse, but the love doesn't change. It deepens.

I don't take this season for granted. Every meal we share, puzzle we work on, every story she tells from decades ago, taking her to doctor appointments, our gambling time at the casino, every moment we have with each other, we're creating a new chapter together—one that's not built on obligation, but on honor.

And when I reflect on the Sacrifice Paradox, I see it clearly here: sometimes, what looks like giving up something of value is, in truth, actually gaining something far more valuable. A deeper connection. A greater understanding. A more meaningful presence.

If you're reading this and you're in a similar season—caring for a parent, a child, a loved one—know this: your presence matters. Your patience matters. And while the sacrifices may go unseen, the legacy you're shaping will outlive all of us.

# 33 Reflection And Growth

As you read the stories in Part II, I encourage you to reflect on your own experiences with sacrifices, and think deeply about the reflection questions posed that truly resonate with you. Consider the choices you have made and the impact they have had on your life. Think about the sacrifices you may need to make in the future and how they align with your values and goals.

The journey of understanding and making sacrifices is deeply personal and unique to everyone. There are no right or wrong answers, only a course of action that resonates with your true self. By embracing the Sacrifice Paradox, you can navigate the complexities of life with greater clarity and purpose.

My hope is that this book will serve as a guide and a source of inspiration as you navigate your own journey of sacrifice and fulfillment.

By the end of this journey, you will have a clear understanding of how to make sacrifices that align with your purpose and values and lead to a more fulfilling life.

Remember, the greatest gains often come from the most significant sacrifices. Embrace the paradox, and you may find that the act of giving up something valuable can lead to the most profound growth and success.

# PART II

# 101 Inspiring Stories Of Sacrifices And Trade-Offs

# 1 The Student's Dilemma

aria was a high school senior with her sights set on a prestigious university. Driven and determined, she crafted color-coded study plans, skipped parties to prep for standardized tests, and spent weekends polishing essays instead of attending dances. While her classmates built memories at football games and bonfires, Maria buried herself in textbooks, convinced that every hour of effort would shape her future.

And it did.

She earned a full scholarship to her dream school, an Ivy League acceptance letter, and she could hardly believe it. Her parents beamed with pride. Her teachers used her as an example. She had achieved exactly what she set out to do.

But as senior year came to a close, Maria found herself watching videos of prom on social media. She scrolled through photos of her classmates at graduation parties, laughing, celebrating, connecting. She realized she didn't have many pictures of her own. No inside jokes from group outings. No stories of nights that turned into mornings. Her academic success had come with a cost.

The *trade-off* was short-term fun for long-term opportunity.

The *benefit* was securing a world-class education and building a foundation for her future.

The *consequence* was a sense of emotional distance, missing out on moments she could never recreate.

Maria didn't regret her choices, but she learned that success isn't just about where you arrive—it's also about what you carry with you along the way.

### Reflection Questions

Have you ever sacrificed joy in the moment for the promise of something greater? Looking back, how did it shape who you are—and what, if anything, would you do differently?

The Kitchen Table
Start-Up

James had what many would call a "good life," a stable job in a respected firm, a reliable paycheck, and the kind of benefits package most people dream of. But every day he sat at his desk, he felt the pull of something more. His passion for emerging tech and innovation buzzed in his mind constantly, and he couldn't shake the feeling that he was meant to build something of his own.

After years of late-night brainstorming, weekend research, and countless "what if" conversations with his closest friends, James made the leap. He left the comfort of his corporate career and poured his life savings into launching a tech start-up based on an idea he had been refining for years.

The early days were incredibly challenging.

He worked from his kitchen table, juggled multiple roles, and lived lean with no vacations, no nights out, and plenty of ramen noodles. He watched friends buy houses while he worried about making payroll. There were moments of self-doubt and near-burnout. The security he once had now felt like a distant memory.

The *trade-off* was between financial safety and betting on himself.

The *benefit* was realizing a long-held dream: his start-up eventually gained traction, attracted investors, and became profitable.

The *consequence* was years of strain on his personal life, missed milestones with loved ones, and the mental toll of carrying risk day after day.

But James never lost sight of why he started. His journey wasn't just about launching a product. It was about reclaiming purpose.

### Reflection Question

If you could remove the risk of failure, what passion project would you pursue today?

# 3   The Mother's Relief

Claire had built a name for herself as a top-tier marketing strategist at a fast-growing startup. She was the person others came to when a campaign needed rescuing, or a brand needed redefining. She loved the pace, the problem-solving, and the creative rush of making something out of nothing.

But after the birth of her second child, the blur between brand meetings and bedtime routines started to wear her down. One afternoon, while reviewing analytics for a major client presentation, she missed a call from her daughter's daycare. Her daughter had fallen and needed stitches. Claire hadn't even seen the missed call until two hours later.

That night, sitting in the kitchen with a glass of wine and a pit in her stomach, Claire made a call of her own. She asked her CEO to take her off the leadership track and transition into a part-time advisory role.

It felt like a betrayal to the team, to her ambition, to the version of herself that had fought to earn every promotion. But it also felt like relief.

The *trade-off* was clear: she gave up her shot at becoming the company's CMO, a role she had envisioned for years.

The *benefit* was the ability to show up fully for her children, to be present, not just in body, but in energy and attention.

The *consequence* was more complicated. A year later, when the company went public, Claire wasn't on the leadership team that rang the bell at the stock exchange. She watched it on a livestream from her kitchen, toddler on her hip, applause echoing through her laptop.

She didn't regret the choice. She just acknowledged the cost.

### Reflection Question

What's the professional milestone you've had to let go of, and what did you gain instead?

# The Invisible War

Marcus was a respected Army officer—disciplined, honorable, and deeply committed to his mission. He wasn't the loudest in the room, but his presence commanded attention. He volunteered for back-to-back deployments not because he sought danger, but because he believed his leadership mattered. He believed in service before self.

But while Marcus fought visible battles abroad, one unfolded at home.

Every deployment meant another missed birthday. Another first day of school without him in the photo. Another school event was watched later on a phone screen. His wife carried the weight of both parents, and his children learned to stop asking when he'd be home.

The *trade-off* was between fulfilling a promise to serve and showing up for the people who needed him most.

The *benefit* was upholding the values he swore to protect freedom, leading with integrity, and supporting his brothers and sisters in uniform.

The *consequence* was a gradual erosion of closeness. When he finally returned home for good, he found himself a stranger in the family photos. His kids were taller. Their routines no longer included him. Rebuilding that connection would take time and humility.

Marcus carried no regrets about serving his country. But he also came to understand that some sacrifices are unseen to others, and they echo long after the mission ends.

### Reflection Questions

Have you ever fulfilled an important obligation while grieving what it cost you at home? How did you begin to heal what distance left behind?

# 5 The All-In Routine

Emily was an elite gymnast with dreams of earning a full-ride scholarship to a top university. From the age of seven, her life revolved around the gym. She trained from dawn until dusk. before school, after school, weekends, holidays. While her classmates went to birthday parties, sleepovers, and school dances, Emily was perfecting routines, taping injuries, and chasing the next level of difficulty.

Her world was discipline, repetition, and pressure.

To pursue her goal, she sacrificed sleep, spontaneity, and the hallmarks of a typical teenage life. No summer road trips. No prom. No weekends off.

The *trade-off* was between personal enjoyment and athletic achievement.

The *benefit* was undeniable: she earned a full athletic scholarship to a Division I university and became a standout on her team.

The *consequence* was more subtle, realizing later that she had very few memories outside of gymnastics and struggled to define herself without a scoreboard.

Years down the line, Emily felt pride in what she accomplished—but also a grief for the girlhood she never really lived.

### Reflection Questions

Have you ever given up personal enjoyment for the sake of a long-term goal? How did it affect you?

STORY
6

# The Bell That Kept Ringing

M r. Johnson wasn't just a teacher. He was the kind of educator students remembered decades later. The one who spotted potential before the student saw it in themselves. Who bought granola bars for kids who skipped breakfast. Who stayed late not because he had to, but because he couldn't imagine sending a kid home feeling like a failure.

What most people didn't see was what he gave up to do it.

His school days didn't end when the bell rang. They ended when the tutoring session was over, when the lesson plans were done, and when the parent emails were answered. And sometimes, when the janitor locked the building for the night.

Weekends, once filled with fishing and pickup basketball, turned into grading marathons and AP prep sessions. Birthdays and anniversaries with his wife were postponed because he was "just too tired." His own kids learned to check his classroom before asking if he was coming home for dinner.

The *trade-off* was significant: personal interests, family rituals, and the mental space to just be "Tom" instead of "Mr. Johnson."

The *benefit* was students who graduated when they almost didn't, letters years later saying, "You changed my life," and knowing he helped launch futures.

The *consequence*, though, lingered. A growing sense that while he poured everything into others, he hadn't left much room for himself.

Even so, if you asked him, he'd probably say, "I didn't get everything right. But I showed up when it mattered."

### Reflection Question

When does commitment turn into overextension, and how do you know when it's time to reclaim something for yourself?

# The Artist's Pursuit

Samantha didn't just paint. She *had* to paint. It was the only way she made sense of the world. Her canvases carried pieces of her that words couldn't reach. But passion alone didn't pay the rent.

After graduating from art school, Samantha turned down a stable graphic design job that would've offered benefits, a steady paycheck, and structure. Instead, she chose to chase her dream of being a full-time painter.

The dream came with reality.

She worked three part-time jobs—dog walking, waiting tables, and teaching beginner art classes—just to cover rent on a tiny studio apartment with cracked tile and paper-thin walls. Her refrigerator was often empty, her social life nearly nonexistent, and she spent more nights washing brushes at 1 a.m. than sleeping eight hours.

Friends bought homes. Traveled. Had health insurance. Samantha, meanwhile, debated whether to buy groceries or a new set of oils.

The *trade-off* was financial stability and social normalcy in exchange for a life rooted in creative expression.

The *benefit* was moments of flow where she felt completely alive, and the pride of knowing her work touched people in small but honest ways.

The *consequence* was missed weddings, overdue bills, and a creeping loneliness she couldn't always paint her way through.

Every time she considered giving it up, something pulled her back to the easel.

### Reflection Question

What has comfort or stability asked you to trade—and was it worth the silence of not trying?

# The Doctor's Dedication

D r. Lee was one of the top cardiothoracic surgeons in the region. Colleagues admired his precision under pressure. Patients spoke of him with reverence. His name was on awards, research papers, and hospital boards. To the outside world, he was a symbol of excellence.

But behind the scenes, the pace was relentless.

Twelve-hour shifts often stretched into sixteen. Holidays became just another day in scrubs. Family dinners were replaced with late-night vending machine meals. His calendar was packed with surgeries, but rarely held space for anniversaries, parent-teacher conferences, or simply time to rest.

Dr. Lee never complained. Saving lives was a calling, and he bore it with pride. But the costs accumulated. His spouse began to feel more like a roommate. His kids stopped expecting him at weekend games. His body, pushed beyond exhaustion, began sending subtle warnings—ignored in the name of service.

The *trade-off* was between professional mastery and personal presence.

The *benefit* was undeniable: lives saved, breakthroughs achieved, a legacy of healing.

But the *consequence* was deep. An aching disconnect from his family, missed memories he could never get back, and a growing awareness that while he was fixing other people's hearts, he had nearly broken his own.

Eventually, Dr. Lee stepped back—not from medicine, but from the belief that sacrifice meant surrendering everything else.

### Reflection Question

When your work demands more than you have to give, how do you protect what matters most outside of your profession?

# 9    The Game He Let Go

Tyler was the kind of athlete who made it look easy. Coaches called him a natural. Scouts circled his name. By senior year, he had a standing offer to join a top-tier development team—one step away from the pros.

But Tyler also had a different kind of gift. He was just as good in a physics lab as he was on the field. He loved problem-solving, building things from scratch, and tinkering until something clicked.

Then came the clash.

The training schedule left no room for his engineering classes. His professors warned him. His coaches told him to pick a lane.

And so, at nineteen, Tyler made a decision that would shape the rest of his life.

He walked away from the sport.

Not because he wasn't good enough, or because he lost the drive, but because he knew he couldn't give both his full effort. And he didn't want to halfway anything.

The *trade-off* was gut-wrenching: the adrenaline of packed stadiums, the possibility of a pro career, the thrill of being *known*.

The *benefit* was structure, stability, and the pride of graduating with honors, and later, designing systems that were actually making a difference.

The *consequence* came every time he watched a match, there was a tug. A flicker of *what if.* A moment where he pictured himself still out there.

He doesn't regret his choice. But he's honest enough to admit that he misses the game.

**Reflection Question**

When you say no to one version of your future, how do you make peace with the one you didn't choose?

# The Weekend Shift

Every Saturday morning, while most of her friends slept in or planned brunch, Helen pulled on sneakers and drove across town to the local homeless shelter. She spent her weekends sorting donations, serving hot meals, and listening—really listening—to stories most people would rather avoid.

Helen never sought praise. She didn't post about her work or ask for recognition. She volunteered because it grounded her. It reminded her of how fragile stability could be—and how much dignity a single act of kindness could restore.

But over time, the weight of her commitment grew heavier.

She began declining weekend invitations. Girls' trips. Family reunions. Even lazy Sunday afternoons. People eventually stopped asking. They admired her dedication, but they also missed her.

The *trade-off* was between replenishing her own social and emotional energy and showing up for those with far greater needs.

The *benefit* was profound: a deep sense of purpose, human connection, and the knowledge that she was making a difference.

The *consequence* was more complicated—friendships that slowly faded, family moments she couldn't get back, and a creeping fatigue that even service couldn't soothe.

Eventually, Helen realized that helping others didn't mean abandoning herself. She began setting aside one weekend a month just for rest or connection, because even those who serve need space to refill their own cup.

### Reflection Question

When giving to others becomes your default, how do you recognize when it's time to give something back to yourself?

# The Corporate Climb

R obert had always been driven. From his first entry-level job to the corner office, he approached his career like a mission. Strategic, relentless, and uncompromising. Promotions came quickly. So did the perks: a six-figure salary, stock options, international travel, and a sleek office overlooking the skyline.

To most, he had "made it."

But the climb came at a cost.

Robert's days bled into nights. Weekends were reserved for catching up on emails. Vacations were either cut short or spent glued to conference calls. He missed recitals, anniversaries, and calm Sunday mornings. His spouse began referring to him as a "visitor" in their own home. His kids stopped asking if he'd be there because they already knew the answer.

The *trade-off* was between relentless professional ascent and the steady erosion of his personal life.

The *benefit* was clear: status, financial freedom, and the validation that came with being indispensable at work.

The *consequence* was more painful. Strained family ties, emotional distance, and the realization that success in one area often demands sacrifice in another.

One night, after closing a major deal, Robert returned to a dark house. No one was waiting up. For the first time, the silence didn't feel peaceful—it felt empty.

### Reflection Question

What does success mean to you—and what are you willing to give up to achieve it?

STORY
12

# The Lane She Left Empty

M egan wasn't just on the swim team. She was the swim team.

Coaches saw her as Olympic material. Teammates counted on her to anchor relays. She loved the water. It gave her focus, discipline, and a sense of control she couldn't find anywhere else.

But as college approached, something shifted. The pressure to stay elite started to take more from her than it gave. The early mornings, the late-night study sessions, the constant fatigue. They didn't just exhaust her; they blurred the edges of who she was outside of a swimsuit and a stopwatch.

Megan found herself asking a question she'd never asked before: *"If I'm not training, who am I?"*

When she received an academic scholarship offer from a university that didn't have a competitive swim program, she hesitated. Could she really walk away from the identity she had carried since she was ten?

After long conversations with her family—and a tear-filled meeting with her coach—she made the call. She chose to leave swimming behind and focus entirely on her academic future.

The *trade-off* wasn't just about time or logistics—it was about letting go of a part of herself that once defined her.

The *benefit* was clarity. Space to explore new passions. A thriving academic life that brought her unexpected joy.

The *consequence* was an ache she felt every time she walked by a pool.

But now, she sees herself as more than a swimmer. She's a writer. A scientist. A leader on campus. And every once in a while, she swims, but on her own terms.

### Reflection Questions

Have you ever had to give up one success for another? How did it affect your future?

# 13 The Musician's Encore

A lex wasn't just good at music. He lived it. From the moment he picked up a guitar in high school, everything else faded into the background. While his peers were downloading playlists, Alex was composing them. When others went out on Friday nights, he was playing open mics at coffee shops, hoping someone—anyone—might hear something worth remembering.

To support his dream, he juggled multiple part-time jobs: stocking shelves at a grocery store, delivering food until midnight, and teaching beginner guitar lessons on weekends. The money barely covered gear, studio time, and the occasional string replacement. Nights out and weekend trips? Not in the budget. Friendships slowly drifted as his focus narrowed.

The *trade-off* was between stability and a shot at turning his passion into a career.

The *benefit* came slowly. His music caught the right ears, and over time, he built a loyal following. Eventually, one of his songs went viral, launching him into the industry with a record deal and sold-out shows.

But the *consequence* was that while he had gained recognition, he had missed out on the messy, joyful, and spontaneous moments that shape young adulthood. His world had been music, but not much else.

He never questioned the path. His journey wasn't just about fame. It was about proving that devotion, even when lonely, can become something beautiful.

### Reflection Questions

Have you ever poured yourself so fully into a goal that other parts of your life faded into the background? What did it cost—and was it worth it?

# 14 The Caregiver

Julia was twenty-eight, ambitious, and on the brink of a major promotion at her consulting firm. She had a five-year plan, a mentor who believed in her, and a steady rhythm of client wins that were making her a rising star.

Then her mother had a stroke.

Suddenly, the woman who once held everything together couldn't manage the stairs, couldn't remember appointments, and couldn't be left alone.

Julia didn't think twice. She packed her apartment into boxes, took a leave of absence "for a few weeks," and moved back home.

Weeks turned into months.

She became a caregiver overnight, ordering medical supplies, administering medications, and managing doctor visits. She slept lightly, always listening for her mom to stir in the night. Friends drifted. Career momentum vanished. Her own life? Paused.

The *trade-off* was immense: the loss of professional identity, financial autonomy, and the social freedom that had once filled her weekends.

The *benefit* was knowing, deep down, that she showed up in the moment that mattered most, offering dignity, presence, and love when her mother needed it most.

The *consequence* was a different kind of grief: not just for the parent she was slowly losing, but for the version of her life she had to let go of, too.

Julia eventually re-entered the workforce, but she was never quite the same, and that, she realized, was the point.

### Reflection Question
What does it cost you to pause your own life for someone else, and what unexpected gifts can come from that pause?

The Scientist's
Protégé

D
r. Patel was leading a project that had the potential to earn her international recognition. Funding was tight, and competition for lab space was fierce. Just as she was finalizing her proposal for a major research grant, she discovered that a promising young scientist in her department was working on a related project, but was about to lose funding altogether.

Patel faced a decision: protect her own proposal and secure her place at the top of the field, or step aside and nominate her protégé for the grant, giving the younger scientist the resources needed to advance their work.

She chose the latter, sacrificing her own shot at prestige to ensure the next generation could carry the research forward.

The *trade-off* was between personal advancement and investing in someone else's success.

The *benefit* was seeing her mentee make a breakthrough that might not have happened otherwise.

The *consequence* was slowing her own career trajectory and wondering how different her path might have been.

### Reflection Question

When faced with a choice, are you willing to put another person's future ahead of your own ambition?

# 16 The Writer's Solitude

Laura had always dreamed of becoming a published novelist. She didn't just want to write. She wanted to create something lasting, something that would move people. But after years of juggling writing with her day job and social obligations, she realized that if her book was ever going to be finished, she needed to make space for it. Real space.

So she took a leap. Laura gave notice at work, sublet her apartment, and retreated to a small cabin tucked away in the mountains. There was no Wi-Fi, no city noise, no late-night texts from friends asking her to meet for drinks: just a desk, a wood-burning stove, and the blinking cursor on her laptop.

The first few days felt like freedom. But as the weeks wore on, the silence grew louder. She missed birthdays. She missed conversations. She missed being needed.

She wrote. She edited. She rewrote entire chapters. She doubted herself, pushed through, and kept going.

The *trade-off* was clear: creative immersion in exchange for personal connection and financial security.

The *benefit* was finally finishing her manuscript. Her novel not only found a publisher but also went on to receive critical acclaim.

The *consequence* was more than loneliness. It was returning home to friendships that had faded, a bank account nearly drained, and the realization that while she had captured her story on paper, she had briefly lost her place in the world around her.

Laura didn't regret the solitude. But she emerged with a new vow. For her next book, she wouldn't disappear to create. She'd bring her life with her.

### Reflection Question

When pursuing something deeply meaningful, how do you stay connected to the people who ground you?

STORY
17

# The Engineer's Innovation

Malik was a brilliant engineer leading a cutting-edge project that had the potential to revolutionize sustainable energy. It was the kind of opportunity professionals dream about—high-impact, high-visibility, and high-stakes. The project demanded everything: long nights at the lab, early morning calls with international partners, and a constant stream of urgent decisions.

Malik became consumed by the mission. He missed family dinners, his daughter's school play, and even his wedding anniversary. His weekends blurred into weekdays. His saxophone collected dust, and friendships slowly faded into unread texts.

The *trade-off* was between professional achievement and personal life.

The *benefit* was significant: Malik's work helped bring a breakthrough product to market. He received industry recognition, speaking invitations, and a promotion.

But the *consequence* was sobering. He felt like a stranger at home, disconnected from the people and passions that once brought him joy.

Only after the project's launch did Malik realize that success had come at a cost he hadn't fully calculated.

### Reflection Question

How do you manage the demands of a high-stakes project while maintaining a connection with loved ones?

STORY
18 The Cause She Carried

C hloe had always been a high achiever. As a corporate lawyer in a prestigious firm, she'd built a reputation for being relentless, sharp, and unstoppable in the courtroom. On paper, she had it all: six-figure income, designer wardrobe, and a corner office looking out on the mountains.

But each morning, as she sipped her coffee scrolling through news about oil spills, vanishing wildlife, and government rollbacks on climate regulations, something gnawed at her. The disconnect between what she fought for professionally and what she cared about personally had become too big to ignore.

So, Chloe made a decision that baffled her colleagues and family alike: she walked away.

She left the firm and accepted a modest role at a grassroots environmental nonprofit. No prestige. No elevator. No more lavish bonuses. Her days were now spent writing grant proposals, speaking at community events, and joining protests with rain-soaked signs. She traded polished courtrooms for muddy trails and corporate dinners for recycled-lunchbox potlucks.

The *trade-off* was that she sacrificed financial security, career momentum, and the professional identity she had carefully built.

The *benefit* was waking up with clarity and purpose, knowing that every ounce of effort now aligned with what mattered most to her.

The *consequence* was that she downsized her lifestyle, faced moments of doubt, and wrestled with feelings of professional invisibility in a world that once applauded her every move.

But when she saw a wetland preserved because of the campaign she helped lead, or when she mentored a young activist ready to take up the torch, she felt something that money never gave her: wholeness.

### Reflection Question

What part of your identity would you be willing to get go of to fight for something you believe in?

# The Final Whistle

avid had spent his entire adult life on the football field. From Friday night lights to Sunday stadium crowds, the game had been his identity, his purpose, his world. He knew the physical toll was part of the job—bruises, concussions, surgeries—but he always bounced back. Until he didn't.

After yet another knee injury and a lingering concussion that affected his memory, David sat in front of a panel of doctors who didn't mince words. One more hit could mean permanent damage, neurological or otherwise.

For the first time, he realized the game he loved might not love him back.

He wrestled with the decision for weeks. His teammates were gearing up for another season. Fans still wore his jersey. Inside the locker room, he felt alive. But he also noticed the way his body tensed climbing stairs, how he forgot small things, how sleep didn't come easily anymore.

The *trade-off* was between continuing to play the sport he loved and protecting his long-term health and future.

The *benefit* was choosing to walk away before he was forced to, preserving his body, his mind, and the possibility of a full life beyond football.

The *consequence* was profound: losing the adrenaline of the game, the daily rhythm of training, the roar of the crowd, and the confidence of knowing exactly who he was.

Retirement wasn't just the end of a career. It was the beginning of an identity crisis.

David eventually found purpose in coaching, mentoring younger athletes, and using his story to advocate for player safety. But even years later, every fall Sunday stirred something in him. A twinge of nostalgia. A reminder of the price he paid to protect what could not be replaced.

### Reflection Question

When something you love begins to take more from you than it gives, how do you find the courage to let it go—and the strength to redefine who you are?

# The Immigrants' Journey

Carlos and Josefina had built meaningful lives in their home country. He was an engineer. She managed a thriving dental clinic. Their days were filled with work they loved, neighbors they trusted, and traditions that anchored their family. But as the political climate grew increasingly unstable, the future began to darken, especially for their children.

What once felt like home now felt like risk.

So, with heavy hearts, they made the decision to leave. They didn't flee in secrecy or desperation. Instead, they applied for legal immigration through the proper channels, a process that required paperwork, background checks, interviews, and a patience that stretched over months. Eventually, they were granted permission to begin again in a new country.

They packed only what would fit in a handful of suitcases, said goodbye to aging parents, and boarded a plane to a place where they knew no one and barely spoke the language.

In their new country, their credentials didn't translate. Degrees were questioned. Experience went unrecognized. Carlos found work in construction. Josefina cleaned office buildings at night. They worked long hours, learned phrases on the bus, and smiled through exhaustion so their children could have a shot at a future they never imagined giving up.

The *trade-off* was between staying in a familiar place with a dimming future or embracing the unknown in pursuit of safety and possibility.

The *benefit* was undeniable: their children thrived in school, learned the new language with ease, and grew up with opportunities their parents could only dream of.

But the *consequence* was deeply felt loneliness, the ache of being unseen, the slow erosion of their professional identities, and the longing for a homeland that still lived in their hearts.

When Carlos watched his daughter cross the stage at her high school graduation, diploma in hand, he turned to Josefina and whispered, "*This is why we came.*"

### Reflection Questions

Have you ever given up something deeply personal for the sake of someone else's future? What did that experience teach you about strength, identity, and love?

# 21 The Reawakening

Anastasia had climbed the corporate ladder with precision and poise. As a senior executive at a global firm, she had everything that defined success. Status, stability, a generous salary, and a lifestyle most people envied. But beneath the surface, something felt off. Meetings felt repetitive. Milestones felt hollow. She craved meaning more than momentum.

Then, a devastating earthquake struck a neighboring country. As news poured in and images of collapsed homes and displaced families flooded her screen, Anastasia felt something shift. Without fully understanding why, she requested a leave of absence from work and signed up with an international relief organization.

Within two weeks, she traded boardrooms for disaster zones. She found herself hauling debris under sweltering sun, coordinating supply drops, comforting families who had lost everything, and sleeping on a cot in a shared shelter. Gone were her routines, conveniences, and polished wardrobe. In their place came blistered hands, aching muscles, and a sense of renewal.

The *trade-off* was clear: personal comfort and professional security for the chance to make a direct, human impact.

The *benefit* was a deep sense of purpose and humility, forged in the service of others.

The *consequence* was stepping away from a promising career and facing the unknown—if her job would be waiting when she returned, or whether she even wanted to return at all.

What Anastasia gained couldn't be measured in performance metrics or bonuses. It was found in shared meals with strangers, handwritten thank-you notes in languages she didn't speak, and the rediscovery of what mattered most.

### Reflection Questions
Would you be willing to leave your comfort zone to have influence in the world? Why or why not?

# The Dream They Gave Away

John and Lisa had finally arrived.

After years of professional advancement, raising three kids, and saving aggressively, they were ready to break ground on the custom lake house they'd dreamed about since their honeymoon. They had the lot. The plans. The down payment.

Then came the curveball: their youngest son, Daniel, who had always struggled with focus and learning, was diagnosed with a complex neurodevelopmental condition. His new educational needs couldn't be met at the local public school—not even close.

There was a private academy across the state that specialized in his exact condition. Full-time enrollment. Small classes. One-on-one support. Life-changing, they were told.

But it came at a price. It wasn't just money, but a shift in their entire lives.

John and Lisa didn't hesitate. They pulled out of the lake house deal. Sold their upscale home. Told their friends they were "downsizing," though the real reason hurt more than their pride would admit. They moved into a two-bedroom condo and took on longer commutes. John even turned down a speaking engagement at a major industry event because of Daniel's therapy schedule.

The *trade-off* wasn't just financial. It was emotional. Letting go of something they had earned, something they had imagined together for decades.

The *benefit* was watching Daniel thrive. He laughed more. Learned more. Stood taller.

The *consequence* was the grief of a dream delayed indefinitely, and the discomfort of watching peers post lake house photos while they struggled with sacrifice behind the scenes.

There was no regret because one day, Daniel said, "I like school now." And that was enough.

### Reflection Questions

When a dream collides with your child's needs, how do you choose? How do you grieve what you gave up?

# STORY 23 The Social Worker's Dedication

N ina didn't choose social work for recognition or a comfortable life. She chose it because she believed every child deserved safety, love, and a second chance. As a caseworker for children in foster care, she carried a caseload that often felt heavier than the hours in a day. But she kept going.

She worked late into the night, wrote court reports from kitchen tables, and made weekend home visits when no one else was available. Holidays were often interrupted by crises. She was the one who answered the phone at 11 p.m., especially when a child was moved unexpectedly or a foster parent felt overwhelmed.

Nina gave everything—her time, her energy, and eventually, pieces of herself.

The stories stayed with her. The children who were reunited with their families. The ones who weren't. The laughter that broke through trauma, and the silence that followed some goodbyes. She carried it all.

The *trade-off* was between preserving her own mental health and showing up consistently for the kids who needed her most.

The *benefit* was lasting. She helped change the trajectory of hundreds of lives. She was a lifeline in moments when others had given up.

The *consequence* was the emotional fatigue, disrupted sleep, and the creeping feeling that her compassion had nowhere left to land.

Eventually, Nina sought therapy. Not because she was weak, but because she realized the strength it takes to care for others must include caring for yourself.

### Reflection Question

What would change if you treated your own well-being as non-negotiable—not after the work is done, but as part of the work itself?

# 24 The Explorer's Path

Timothy had always felt restless behind a desk. While his job offered security and a predictable path forward, each day felt like a page torn from someone else's story. The routines dulled him, and the spark he once had began to fade.

One evening, he made a decision that had been building inside him for years: he was going to leave it all behind.

He sold most of what he owned, broke the lease on his apartment, and booked a one-way ticket abroad. With a well-worn backpack, a tattered journal, and no concrete plan, he set out to chase a different kind of wealth—experience.

His journey took him across winding mountain trails in Nepal, into lantern-lit markets in Morocco, and through sunrises in the Andes. He shared meals with strangers, got lost in unfamiliar languages, and found comfort in the simplicity of a life lived in motion.

The *trade-off* was between the comfort of stability and the thrill of the unknown.

The *benefit* was a life rich with stories, perspective, and a deep understanding of how much we all share, regardless of language or latitude.

But the *consequence* lingered too: missed birthdays, an empty savings account, and moments of aching solitude. He often wondered what it would feel like to have a place that felt like *home* again.

Timothy never saw his journey as an escape. It was a pursuit, not of places, but of meaning.

**Reflection Questions**

Have you ever chosen freedom over familiarity? What did you discover about the world—or yourself—when you stepped off the map?

136

The Innovator's
Isolation

E than wasn't chasing attention. He wasn't trying to be
the next big name in tech. He just believed in the
problem he was solving, and the elegant, powerful
solution he'd mapped out in his head.

It started innocently enough. Late nights in the garage,
prototypes drawn on napkins, missed calls that he promised
to return later. But "later" kept slipping further away.

As the weeks turned into months, Ethan slowly
disappeared from the lives of people who once anchored
him. Friends stopped inviting him out. His sister joked
that he only existed in the group chat. Even his partner,
who once cheered on his ambition, began to grow distant.

But Ethan kept pushing. The algorithm worked. The
product took shape. The investors came. It launched.
Headlines were written.

He had built something brilliant.

The *trade-off* was total: he sacrificed not only his social life and relationship but also his physical and emotional well-being.

The *benefit* was undeniable. His invention changed workflows across an entire industry and gave him financial security for the first time in his life.

The *consequence* was deeper than loneliness. It was the hollow feeling of success without celebration, of winning something with no one left to share it with.

Only after the noise faded did he realize he hadn't just built a product. He had built a tunnel. And he had to figure out how to come back through it.

### Reflection Question

What are you building, and will the people you care about still be there when you're done?

# The College Graduate's Gamble

J ulian had just walked across the graduation stage with a degree in engineering and a job offer already in hand. It was everything he had worked for: high income, relocation assistance, and a prestigious firm with a fast track to advancement. Everyone around him celebrated. Everyone assumed he'd take it.

But Julian had a different dream pulling at him.

During his final semester, he and a few classmates had developed a prototype for a sustainability-focused tech product. It wasn't perfect, but it had potential. When their concept was accepted into a competitive start-up incubator program in his hometown, Julian found himself at a crossroads.

Take the safe path or bet on the uncertain one.

Julian turned down the corporate offer and moved into a shared apartment with two co-founders. He lived off a modest stipend, poured his energy into pitch decks and product iterations, and stayed up late chasing the spark that had once been just an idea on a napkin.

The *trade-off* was between financial stability and the uncertain pursuit of passion.

The *benefit* was autonomy, purpose, and the thrill of building something from the ground up.

The *consequence* was sleepless nights, moments of doubt, near-empty bank accounts, and the fear that he had made the wrong choice.

But through the chaos, Julian found clarity not just about his product, but about himself. He learned that success isn't always measured by a salary, but by the courage to follow a path no one else can see but you.

### Reflection Questions

Have you ever said no to something secure in order to say yes to something meaningful? What helped you decide—and what did the risk reveal?

# 27 The Grandparent's Gift

**M**argaret had dreamed for years of traveling the world once she retired. She had maps marked with places she hoped to visit: Italy's coastlines, the tulip fields of the Netherlands, and the train routes through the Canadian Rockies. Her suitcase was packed, figuratively speaking, even before her final day of work.

But when her granddaughter, Agnes, was accepted into her top-choice university, the reality of tuition costs came crashing down. Scholarships only covered part of it, and loans would leave Agnes burdened for decades.

Margaret had a decision to make.

Without fanfare or second-guessing, she offered a portion of her retirement savings to cover the remaining costs. She never framed it as a sacrifice. In her words, *"Travel can wait. Futures can't."*

The *trade-off* was between fulfilling her own lifelong travel dreams and giving her granddaughter a debt-free start in life.

The *benefit* was watching Agnes thrive. Graduating with honors, landing her dream job, and growing into the confident woman Margaret always believed she could be.

The *consequence* was letting go of long-held plans and accepting that some of her own dreams might remain unfulfilled.

But when Agnes crossed the graduation stage and later thanked her with tears in her eyes and a hug that lingered, Margaret knew this, too, was an adventure, and one worth every penny.

---

### Reflection Questions

How far would you go to support a loved one's education or future? What would you be willing to give up?

# 28 The Yes She Didn't Say

**M**ia was on a fast leadership track. Three years into her role at a high-performing marketing firm, she'd just been tapped for a senior account executive position. The new role came with a raise, more visibility, and the kind of career momentum she had always wanted.

But it also came with constant travel.

Three cities a week. Tight timelines. Virtual meetings from airport lounges. It would be exciting, no doubt, but exhausting, too. And it meant she'd be away more than home, just as she and her fiancé were trying to plan their wedding. They'd already postponed it once due to work demands.

Mia sat with the offer letter longer than she expected. She stared at the numbers, the bullet points, the congratulatory note from the VP.

Then she closed her laptop.

She declined the promotion.

Not because she lacked ambition. But because she finally saw how often she'd pushed life to the edges of her calendar. And this time, she didn't want to squeeze her relationship between business trips and late-night proposals.

The *trade-off* was that she sacrificed short-term advancement and the fast track she had worked so hard to earn.

The *benefit* was a steadier home life, a deeper connection, and being present for one of the most meaningful chapters in her personal life.

The *consequence* was feeling a little sidelined at work, watching someone else take the lead she had earned, and wondering, some nights, if she'd made a mistake.

But when she walked down the aisle months later, without checking her phone once that morning, she knew: she had said yes to the right thing.

### Reflection Question

Have you ever said no to something impressive in order to say yes to something important?

# The Classroom Virtuoso

Ms. Franklin had taught music at a small public school for nearly two decades. Her classroom walls were lined with faded concert posters and student drawings of instruments they one day hoped to play. She believed deeply in the power of music, not just as a subject, but as a lifeline for kids who needed something steady, expressive, and their own.

Over time, she noticed a pattern. Some of her most passionate students, the ones who lit up when they talked about rhythm and melody, couldn't afford their own instruments. The school's budget was thin, and the music program was often the first in line for cuts.

So she made a choice.

Without announcement or expectation, Ms. Franklin dipped into her personal savings and bought a few used instruments: a trumpet, two clarinets, a violin, and a pair of drum pads. Then she bought more. Students who had once just watched now held their own tools for expression. Their confidence grew. So did their commitment.

The *trade-off* was between her own financial security and investing in someone else's future.

The *benefit* was watching her students thrive and auditioning for regional ensembles, composing original pieces, and discovering a sense of belonging through music.

The *consequence* was felt later, when she postponed repairs to her car, declined a summer trip she had long planned, and dipped into her emergency fund more than once.

Ms. Franklin never regretted her decision. But she hoped someone would remember that sometimes, the people who make the biggest difference are the ones who give consistently, and at personal cost.

### Reflection Question

When giving to others, how do you draw the line between generosity and self-sacrifice—and what helps you find that balance?

# 30 The Match

O livia wasn't just a tennis player; she was a star. Known for her relentless backhand and fierce focus, she had climbed the rankings faster than anyone expected. Sponsors called. Journalists followed, and her name began to appear on prediction lists for the next Grand Slam.

Then came the match.

It was a high-stakes semifinal, streamed to a global audience. Late in the third set, tied in games, Olivia's opponent served. The ball hit near the line. The umpire hesitated, then called it out. It was game point for Olivia.

But Olivia had seen it. The ball was in.

She stood frozen for a moment, racket by her side, heart pounding. She glanced at her coach, who motioned to keep playing. The crowd roared. Her opponent looked gutted.

Olivia walked to the chair umpire and whispered, "*That ball was in. It's not my point.*"

A hush swept the stadium.

The *trade-off* was immediate: she gave up a pivotal point in the most important match of her career.

The *benefit* was something less tangible but far more lasting. She protected her integrity, earning respect that no trophy could match.

The *consequence* was losing the match. She didn't make the finals. Some fans questioned her judgment, though many praised her. She knew she had likely changed the trajectory of her career with a single choice.

But Olivia slept that night without replaying the point in her mind. She didn't second-guess. She knew she had won something else. Something only she could see.

### Reflection Questions

Have you ever decided to protect your values, even when no one else would have known the difference? What did you risk, and what did you keep?

# The Intervention That Couldn't Wait

J erry had built his company from the ground up. Late nights, calculated risks, and relentless drive. The business was thriving. Clients respected him. His team relied on him.

But things at home told a different story.

His teenage son, Ryan, had begun acting out: slipping grades, school suspensions, emotional outbursts. Teachers flagged concerns. Therapists suggested deeper intervention. His wife confided that Ryan often asked, "*Why is Dad always too busy for me?*"

Jerry heard those words like a gut punch.

He looked at the numbers, the projections, the meetings on his calendar. Then he looked at his son—and realized success in one part of life meant nothing if it came at the cost of another.

Jerry made the hardest decision of his career: he handed over day-to-day control of the company to his most trusted partner. He cleared his schedule. He started showing up not just physically, but fully, for school conferences, therapy sessions, late-night talks, and dinners.

The *trade-off* was between pushing for continued business growth and pressing pause to focus on his family.

The *benefit* was unmistakable: a stronger bond with his son, early intervention that changed Ryan's trajectory, and the rediscovery of his role as a father, not just a provider.

The *consequence* was a slowed pace at work, missed opportunities, and a company that plateaued instead of expanding.

But Jerry never doubted the decision. Because while his business could be rebuilt, his relationship with his son had a window that would not stay open forever.

### Reflection Question

How do you prioritize your family's needs against the demands of your career?

# 32 The Cost Of Discovery

D r. Thompson wasn't in it for the accolades. He was chasing a cure for a rare autoimmune disease that had no name on billboards, no corporate sponsorship, and very little funding. But he believed in the work and the patients waiting for hope.

So he worked. Harder than anyone around him. Nights blurred into mornings under fluorescent lights. Holidays were spent in the lab, not at the dinner table. He missed his daughter's dance recital. His anniversary dinner became a rain check. He told himself, "Just a few more months. Just until the trial data comes in."

But those months stretched into years.

The *trade-off* was clear: he exchanged family memories, rest, and presence for petri dishes, test subjects, and grant reports.

The *benefit* was that his research led to a breakthrough treatment that extended the lives of thousands and opened new doors in immunotherapy.

The *consequence* was personal. A subdued home, a strained marriage, and a teenage son who started turning to his coach instead of his father for advice.

When the FDA finally approved the treatment, Dr. Thompson was handed a plaque. The media called him a hero. He smiled for the photos, proud, but also aware of what he had missed along the way.

### Reflection Question

How do you balance the pursuit of a significant goal with the responsibilities of family life?

# The Couple's Financial Decision

Bianca and Bart had spent years saving, sacrificing dinners out, skipping vacations, and working extra hours, all for one shared dream: buying their first home. They had narrowed down neighborhoods, toured open houses, and even picked out paint colors for the nursery they hoped would come next.

Then everything changed.

Bianca was unexpectedly laid off. Around the same time, her parents, already struggling with medical bills, found themselves in deeper financial trouble after a series of unforeseen expenses. The timing couldn't have been worse.

With a down payment ready in the bank and a pre-approval letter in hand, Bianca and Bart sat at the kitchen table and faced a decision that would redefine their plans.

They chose family.

Instead of moving into a home of their own, they used their savings to help Bianca's parents get back on their feet, paying off medical debt, covering rent, and giving them breathing room to stabilize.

The *trade-off* was painful, pressing pause on their long-awaited milestone to carry someone else's burden.

The *benefit* was the deep relief they brought to people they loved, and the  strength that grew between them as a couple.

The *consequence* was the emotional weight of putting their dream on hold and the uncertainty of when they'd get the chance again.

But when asked if they'd do it differently, Bart simply said, "*A house can wait. Their security couldn't.*"

### Reflection Question

When your plans collide with your values, what helps you decide which path to follow?

# 34 The Framed Path

L ily was a gifted painter with a bold, abstract style that turned heads in local galleries. Her dream had always been to create full-time, living in a loft studio, experimenting without limits, and one day launching her own exhibit series. That dream felt within reach when she was offered a spot in a prestigious artist residency program in Berlin. It came with a stipend, studio space, and international exposure.

But there was a complication: Lily had just been offered a full-time job as a graphic designer at a growing agency in her city. It wasn't her dream, but it came with health insurance, a steady paycheck, and proximity to her friends and long-term partner, who had just signed a lease.

Lily stood at a creative crossroads: take the leap toward artistic uncertainty or choose the path of financial and relational stability.

After weeks of soul-searching, she chose the agency job.

The *trade-off* was between artistic freedom and long-term security.

The *benefit* was building a stable life, staying close to her support system, and sharpening new creative skills.

The *consequence* was shelving a once-in-a-lifetime opportunity to immerse herself in art without boundaries, and wondering, some nights, what might have been.

Years later, Lily still painted. But her definition of success had shifted from chasing prestige to creating on her own terms, in her own time.

### Reflection Questions

Have you ever chosen stability over your passion? What shaped that decision—and how do you feel about it now?

# The Student's Financial Verdict

J ames was a hardworking college student juggling part-time jobs to fund his education. After years of careful saving, he had finally accumulated enough to fulfill a lifelong dream: spending a semester abroad in Europe, immersing himself in new cultures and broadening his global perspective.

But just weeks before finalizing his plans, James received devastating news. His younger sister required emergency surgery, and their family's finances were stretched thin. Without hesitation, James offered up his savings to help cover the cost. He never even mentioned the study abroad trip to his sister.

The *trade-off* was deeply personal: James gave up a once-in-a-lifetime educational opportunity to support a loved one in crisis.

The *benefit* was meaningful: his sister received the care she needed, and their bond grew stronger through the act of sacrifice.

The *consequence* was harder to process. James missed out on cultural experiences, global networking, and the growth that might have come from stepping outside his comfort zone. There were moments of regret, especially when friends posted photos from their own international adventures.

James never questioned his decision. What he lost in experience, he gained in character, and in doing so, discovered a definition of success that had nothing to do with passports or plane tickets.

### Reflection Question

Which personal sacrifices have brought you the greatest meaning?

# The Community Leader's Commitment

**K**aren was a passionate community organizer who had spent over a decade working to revitalize the once-neglected neighborhood where she grew up. She coordinated clean-up projects, fought for small business grants, and launched a local mentorship program for teens. Over time, people began referring to her as "the glue" that held the block together.

But the glue was cracking.

Karen often skipped family gatherings, forgot birthdays, and stopped painting, a hobby she once used to recharge. Her evenings were spent in town hall meetings or writing grant proposals. Her weekends disappeared into street festivals, fundraisers, and last-minute emergencies.

She loved the work. It mattered deeply. But she started to notice a growing hollowness, like she was building something beautiful while slowly disappearing behind it.

The *trade-off* was between personal nourishment and public impact.

The *benefit* was tangible: reduced crime rates, local pride, thriving youth programs, and generations of lives touched.

The *consequence* was personal depletion that strained family ties, emotional fatigue, and the loss of her own passions.

Karen never stopped serving. But eventually, she learned to carve out protected time for long walks, her paintbrush, and the people who missed "just Karen," not "Karen the community leader."

**Reflection Questions**

Would you sacrifice your personal time and interests to serve your community? Why or why not?

# The Story He Didn't Run

Donald had worked for over a decade to earn his seat on the investigative desk. Long hours, risky assignments, and relentless pursuit of the truth had finally led him to a career-defining scoop. A scandal involving a prominent public figure that, if published, would make headlines across the country.

His editor was eager. The pressure was on. "We have enough," she insisted. "If we don't run it now, someone else will."

But Donald wasn't sure. A key source had gone silent, and a document that could confirm everything hadn't yet been authenticated. Without it, the story leaned more on implication than fact. And implication wasn't good enough, not when reputations, livelihoods, and lives were at stake.

Donald made the call to hold the piece.

The newsroom buzzed with frustration. His editor warned him: "*If this breaks elsewhere, you'll own the fallout.*"

The *trade-off* was clear: professional prestige and career momentum versus holding the line on truth and integrity.

The *benefit* was knowing he stayed true to the principles that brought him to journalism in the first place.

The *consequence* was another outlet broke the story days later, and Donald's was seen as a missed opportunity. Rumors of being "too cautious" followed him, and his future at the paper grew uncertain.

Donald had no regrets. He hadn't just protected a story. He had protected what the role was meant to represent: trust, responsibility, and restraint.

Sometimes, the most powerful decision a journalist can make is the one not to publish.

### Reflection Questions

Have you ever had to make a choice between professional advancement and personal ethics? How did you decide?

# The Bridge Between Worlds

A nwar and Fatima weren't fleeing violence or seeking asylum. Their decision to leave their homeland wasn't born of immediate danger—it was born of heartbreak.

Their daughter, Layla, was brilliant. At just twelve, she was building electronics from scraps and dreaming of becoming an aerospace engineer. But in their country, Layla's opportunities as a girl in STEM were limited, her talents dismissed as "a phase." Anwar saw it in the way teachers overlooked her. Fatima felt it in the silence when they asked about advanced classes. They knew if they stayed, the ceiling would close in on her before she ever reached it.

So they made the hardest decision of their lives.

They left behind a modest but stable life, saying goodbye to familiar streets, relatives, and the small business Anwar had spent a decade building. They sold their home, and packed what they could.

This wasn't a desperate escape. It was a strategic, painful, hopeful leap.

They enrolled Layla in a school with a robotics team. Fatima worked nights cleaning offices. Anwar took a job in a warehouse, using hands that once crafted fine furniture to lift crates and sweep floors. They smiled through mispronounced names, navigated paperwork they barely understood, and mourned the life they had left behind.

The *trade-off* was profound: their personal comfort and identity in exchange for their daughter's freedom to become who she was meant to be.

The *benefit* was watching Layla soar, winning science competitions, earning scholarships, and speaking with the confidence they had never dared to model themselves.

The *consequence* was a deep grief. The kind that comes not from regret, but from knowing you may never fully belong again.

As Layla stepped onto a stage to accept her first engineering award, she looked back and mouthed, "*Thank you*." And in that moment, Anwar and Fatima knew: they hadn't lost everything. They had built a bridge—and their daughter had crossed it.

---

### Reflection Questions

What invisible sacrifices have you made to help someone else rise? How do you honor what you've let go of?

# 39 The Chosen Role

Martha was in her early fifties, finally hitting her stride. Her kids had left for college, she had just landed a flexible consulting role, and for the first time in decades, she had weekends to herself. She dreamed of travel, rekindling friendships, and maybe even learning to play the cello.

Then came the call.

Her teenage niece, Ava, had been taken into foster care after years of instability at home. The caseworker asked if Martha would consider temporary guardianship. "Just a few months," they said. "Until things stabilize."

Martha agreed without hesitation, but "temporary" turned into years.

She became a guardian again, navigating curfews, high school chaos, therapy appointments, and late-night heart-to-hearts with a girl who didn't trust adults easily.

Vacations vanished. Her social life slowed. Her flexible job became a lifeline she often juggled during PTA meetings.

The *trade-off* was between a long-awaited season of freedom and stepping back into full-time caregiving.

The *benefit* was offering her niece stability, safety, and unconditional love, breaking a generational cycle in the process.

The *consequence* was shelving her own dreams once more and missing a version of midlife that would never come to be.

Martha never looked back. Some seasons, she learned, aren't about reclaiming time, but about *redeeming* it.

### Reflection Question

How do you decide when to put your own life on hold to care for a loved one?

# The Bridge She Tried To Build

Tara worked as a senior operations director for a global consumer goods company with a less-than-stellar environmental record. The industry had long been criticized for its packaging waste and energy consumption, and Tara knew it.

But unlike some of her colleagues who compartmentalized, Tara didn't look away. She believed meaningful change wasn't just about protest. It was about persistence, influence, and knowing when to push from within.

She stayed.

For a while, it worked. She launched a task force on sustainability. She convinced leadership to test biodegradable materials in one pilot region. She mentored younger employees who wanted to challenge the status quo but didn't know how.

But every step forward came with resistance. Cost concerns. Brand hesitation. Bureaucratic stall-outs. And while Tara was respected, she was often seen as "the green conscience." Useful, but not mission-critical.

The *trade-off* was measured. She kept her salary, her stability, her platform, but accepted slower wins, frustration, and moments of moral fatigue.

The *benefit* was having a seat at the table when key decisions were made, and nudging the company toward more responsible practices, even if the progress was incremental.

The *consequence* was that she sometimes wondered if the pace of internal change would ever catch up with the urgency she felt. She saw peers leave for purpose-driven jobs and wrestled with whether staying made her complicit or courageous.

When a major packaging redesign finally launched with her sustainability specs approved, Tara felt something she hadn't in a long time: momentum.

She hadn't changed the whole system. But she had changed something.

### Reflection Questions

Can real transformation happen from within? How long are you willing to wait for it?

The Unexpected
Journey

After thirty-five years of early mornings, work deadlines, and careful saving, George and Elaine were ready for the next chapter. Retirement had been their long-anticipated prize. An open passport, a bucket list, and time that finally belonged to them.

They had plans: hiking in Patagonia, sipping wine in Tuscany, visiting historic sites across Asia. Their suitcases were bought. Their vaccinations were scheduled.

But just two months in, life took a different turn.

Their daughter, recently divorced and overwhelmed by new motherhood, called in tears. The stress of balancing work, childcare, and emotional recovery was wearing her thin. Without hesitation, George and Elaine offered to help, not temporarily, but full-time. They moved closer, rearranged their days around nap schedules and pediatrician appointments, and traded plane tickets for picture books.

The *trade-off* wasn't just between travel and family. It was between a vision of retirement they had clung to for years and a version of life they hadn't expected.

The *benefit* was a gift they never saw coming: the joy of watching their granddaughter grow up day by day, building a bond few grandparents ever get the chance to have.

The *consequence* was bittersweet. Some destinations were crossed off the list. Time passed, and some dreams dimmed. But something else took their place. Small hands reaching for theirs, milestones witnessed, love deepened.

Over time, they stopped calling it a sacrifice. It became something else: a journey of its own.

### Reflection Question

When life rewrites your plans, how do you find purpose in the path you didn't choose?

## STORY 42 The Career Intermission

B arb was on a meteoric rise in her field. She was an award-winning researcher at one of the top universities in the country. She had just been invited to lead an international research team in Copenhagen, a role that would catapult her into global recognition. Her mentors were thrilled. Her CV was stacked. Everything was lining up.

Except her internal world was falling apart.

After years of saying yes to everything, such as panels, publications, and postdocs, Emily felt hollow. Burned out. Disconnected. She had become a passenger in her own life, saying the right things while craving a pause.

So she did the unthinkable.

She turned down the role and took a year-long sabbatical. No one was sick. No family emergency. She just needed to breathe.

She moved back to her hometown, volunteered at the library, taught a community class, and reconnected with her college roommate over weekly coffee. She read novels again. She napped. She cried. She came back to herself.

The *trade-off* was between accelerated professional prestige and personal clarity.

The *benefit* was rediscovering joy, rest, and relationships untethered to ambition.

The *consequence* was a slower reentry into her field, puzzled colleagues, and a sense of falling off the radar.

But when Emily returned, she brought more than research. She brought presence and a new definition of achievement.

### Reflection Questions

Have you ever chosen to pause—not for crisis, but for clarity? What did stepping back allow you to see more clearly?

# The Space They Chose Not To Share

Marvin and Emily had been married for just six months when the request came.

Marvin's mother asked if they would be willing to move into her home for a short time, she said, to help her adjust to life after her husband's passing. She was lonely, and the house felt too silent. The idea of living with family aligned with the cultural expectations Marvin had grown up with. His mother had taken care of everyone else her whole life. Now, she needed them.

It was a generous request. And a heavy one.

Marvin and Emily had just found their rhythm as a couple. Late-night takeout, messy morning routines, shared dreams of their first apartment filled with mismatched furniture and music playing in the kitchen. Moving in with his mother would mean surrendering that space. Privacy. Autonomy. The ability to build a life that was truly theirs.

After many long conversations and some tears, they made the painful decision to kindly decline.

The *trade-off* was between honoring a parent's emotional need and protecting the fragile foundation of their own new life together.

The *benefit* was the strength of their marriage, rooted in honest dialogue, emotional boundaries, and mutual respect.

The *consequence* was a strained relationship with Marvin's mother. There were awkward holidays, unreturned calls, and guilt that lingered far longer than either of them anticipated.

But what they protected was sacred: the space to grow as partners, not caretakers. And over time, Marvin's mother understood that love doesn't always look like moving in. It can also look like showing up, calling often, and allowing room for something new to take root.

### Reflection Question

When you're pulled between honoring where you come from and protecting what you're building, how do you decide what takes priority?

# The Social Entrepreneur's Crossing

Sophie had spent over a decade in corporate leadership, mastering contracts, negotiations, and long, jargon-filled email threads. Her paycheck was solid. Her future was lined with title upgrades and performance bonuses.

But during a rare vacation abroad, something shifted. She visited a rural community where clean water wasn't a guarantee; it was a privilege. Children walked miles with buckets. Illness from contaminated wells was routine. What hit her hardest wasn't the conditions. It was how distant the problem was to people back home.

When she returned, the fluorescent lighting in her office felt harsher. The documents on her desk felt hollow. The high-profile cases no longer sparked anything inside her.

She resigned three months later.

Sophie launched a social enterprise aimed at bringing sustainable water solutions to underserved communities.

It wasn't glamorous. She traded her high-rise office for crowded airport terminals, unpredictable fundraising cycles, and days that started early and ended late.

The *trade-off* was profound: financial stability, career prestige, and the predictable comforts of the professional world she once thrived in.

The *benefit* was purpose. Raw, daily, and deeply personal. Watching families turn on a clean tap for the first time. Seeing hope where there had only been risk.

The *consequence* was navigating years of financial anxiety, personal doubt, and the grind of building something from scratch without the cushion she'd once enjoyed.

And yet, Sophie never looked back because once she saw the problem, she couldn't unsee it.

### Reflection Question
What would you be willing to leave behind to help solve a problem the world tends to ignore?

# The Stage He Walked Away From

Daniel had always imagined himself on stage, not for fame, not for fans, but for the music—raw, emotional, healing. After years of open mics and independent recordings, he was on the brink of something bigger. He had been invited to audition for a nationally televised talent competition, an opportunity that could finally launch his music career.

But the week before his audition, his younger sister's life unraveled.

A sudden health crisis. Hospital stays. A single parent trying to hold things together. She had always been his biggest supporter, the one who scraped together cash for his first acoustic guitar, the one who sat in every folding chair gig he played.

She needed help. Not just emotional support, but someone to take her son to school, manage late-night shifts, and navigate a swirl of appointments and paperwork.

Daniel looked at the audition form. Then at his calendar. Then at his nephew, asleep on the couch with his music playing through tiny earbuds.

He didn't go to the audition.

The *trade-off* wasn't between creative control and commercial success. It was between chasing a dream and choosing to be present for someone who once did the same for him.

The *benefit* was deeper than a record deal. He gave stability to his family when they needed it most, and music still found its way into the spaces in between.

The *consequence* was heartbreaking. He watched others rise. He sometimes wondered what might have been. But the melody he wrote during that year, the one he sang to his nephew at bedtime, became the song that healed them both.

Daniel never stopped being an artist. He just chose a different audience.

### Reflection Questions

Have you ever put a personal dream on hold to support someone else's? What did that decision cost—and what did it reveal about the kind of legacy you want to leave?

# The Recalibration

aura was a high-performing strategist. She was known for her precision, her client relationships, and her ability to juggle multiple priorities without missing a beat. But what most people didn't see was that Laura was also a single mother.

Her daughter, Chloe, had always been bright and independent. But in middle school, things began to shift. Missed homework, frequent stomachaches, and teary mornings before school. Teachers hinted at anxiety. Laura saw it in the way Chloe avoided eye contact at dinner, how she lingered silently in doorways.

The final push came during a parent-teacher conference when Chloe's math teacher said, "She often seems like she's waiting for something or someone to notice."

Laura noticed.

She made a decision few in her position would dare: she stepped off the fast track, not out of failure, but out of love. She reduced her hours to part-time consulting, turned down a promotion, and cleared her evenings. Colleagues were surprised. Some congratulated her. Others didn't know what to say.

The *trade-off* was complex. Letting go of a hard-earned trajectory for the uncertain reward of emotional presence.

The *benefit* was transformative. Chloe's grades stabilized, her confidence returned, and the two built routines that grounded them both.

The *consequence* was financial pressure, professional momentum slowed, and the haunting fear that future employers might one day see a "gap" instead of a decision rooted in strength.

But Laura knew better. She didn't step away—she stepped *into* the part of life that mattered most at that moment.

### Reflection Question

When faced with a decision between visibility in the world and presence at home, what helps you choose the version of success that matters most?

The Exit Plan
That Saved Her

M s. Green had always been *that* teacher—the one who arrived early, stayed late, and somehow knew what was going on in every student's life. Her classroom was a sanctuary. She bought supplies with her own money, ran after-school clubs, and never missed a school event. Colleagues called her a lifer. Parents called her a saint.

But after ten years, something started to shift.

She found herself dreading Mondays. She couldn't sleep. She snapped at friends and began canceling plans outside of work. It wasn't one moment that broke her. It was the weight of accumulated heartbreak: students going hungry, kids disappearing mid-year, families in crisis with no easy answers. She was burning out. And no one seemed to notice because she was still smiling in the hallway.

Then one afternoon, after a student asked her gently, "*Are you okay, Ms. Green?*" She wasn't sure how to answer.

That night, she made a decision that shocked everyone: she turned in her resignation.

But she didn't leave teaching. She reinvented it.

Ms. Green launched a nonprofit that trained community mentors to work alongside students and families, bridging the gap between school and home. Her hours became manageable. Her joy returned. And her impact multiplied, not because she stayed in one classroom, but because she changed how classrooms could be supported.

The *trade-off* wasn't between staying or leaving. It was between depletion and sustainability.

The *benefit* was reclaiming her well-being while building something that could help more people than she ever imagined.

The *consequence* was grieving the identity she had once wrapped around her job, and accepting that walking away wasn't failure. It was evolution.

### Reflection Questions

When giving becomes draining, how do you know when it's time to step back? How might stepping back actually expand your impact?

STORY
## 48 The Quiet Shift

N athan had built his identity around achievement. He was a partner at a thriving consultancy, leading multi-million-dollar accounts and mentoring a growing team. His calendar was packed, his reputation sterling, and his lifestyle comfortably luxurious.

But as national conversations around inequality, racial justice, and systemic injustice intensified, Nathan found himself unsettled. What began as reading, listening, and attending community forums became a growing discomfort with how detached his professional world felt from the realities so many others lived.

One day, after walking past a peaceful protest on his way to a client dinner, he realized: he didn't just want to donate or post. He wanted to do!

Over the next year, Nathan slowly stepped away from his firm. No dramatic exit, no headlines. Just a deliberate unraveling of a former life to make room for something harder and more personal. He joined a grassroots justice organization as a strategist and advocate, leveraging his skills in the service of something bigger than quarterly growth.

The *trade-off* was between personal success and standing shoulder to shoulder with communities pushing for lasting change.

The *benefit* was the fulfillment of fighting for equity and human dignity, work that aligned with the values he once only discussed privately.

The *consequence* was a dramatic drop in income, professional status, and a few strained friendships from those who couldn't understand why he'd "walk away from everything."

But Nathan hadn't walked away. He had finally walked toward what mattered most to him.

### Reflection Questions

Have you ever felt pulled to step away from what's familiar in order to stand for what's right? What held you back—or pushed you forward?

The Departure They
Didn't Understand

Caroline had just finished college with a modest savings account and a meticulously planned backpacking itinerary. Six countries, three months, and a solo journey she had dreamed of since her sophomore year.

But the moment she announced her departure, the questions began.

"Now's not a good time, is it?"

"Your sister just had a baby. She'll need help."

"Grandma's getting older. You might regret missing time with her."

"You'll travel later, right? After you settle down."

Caroline felt the pressure mounting. Her loved ones weren't in crisis, but they subtly suggested that her leaving was selfish, inconvenient, even irresponsible.

She considered canceling. Postponing. Shrinking the trip.

But something deep inside pushed back: *If not now, when?*

So, she left.

The *trade-off* wasn't between supporting someone in crisis and pursuing a dream. It was between meeting others' expectations and honoring a promise she had made to herself.

The *benefit* was huge: confidence, clarity, new friendships, and a broader worldview that changed how she saw herself and her future.

The *consequence* was lingering guilt, passive-aggressive comments from relatives, and a sense of emotional distance from those who didn't understand why she chose to go.

Caroline returned changed, not just by the places she saw, but by the boundary she set. For the first time, she had chosen herself. And she had no regrets.

### Reflection Questions

Have you ever made a choice others didn't support because it honored something inside you? What did that decision cost, and what did it give back?

## STORY 50  The Corner Office He Let Go

Kevin was a senior engineer with thirty years under his belt, and a solid reputation for solving problems others couldn't touch. So when his company offered him a major promotion, a director role with global scope, it was no surprise. The catch? He'd need to relocate halfway across the country.

It wasn't just about a new office. It was uprooting. New routines. A new zip code. And it would mean leaving behind something far more important: his son, daughter-in-law, and the grandbaby he had just started rocking to sleep on Sunday afternoons.

The old Kevin from ten years ago might have jumped at the chance. But life had changed. He wasn't chasing title upgrades anymore. He was chasing meaning. And those giggles from his granddaughter? They mattered more than the glass-walled office waiting for him in Seattle.

So, Kevin turned it down.

The *trade-off* was visible. Passing on the last big leap in his career and watching as a colleague stepped into the spotlight instead.

The *benefit* was the life he stayed present for—impromptu dinners, birthday parties, soccer games, and a little voice that learned to say "Grandpa" without FaceTime.

The *consequence* was that he sometimes wondered how the role would've shaped him. Whether there was one more mountain left to climb. But those questions disappeared every time his granddaughter crawled into his lap.

## Reflection Question

How do you measure the value of proximity, presence, and shared moments against professional milestones?

## STORY 51 — The Portfolio She Closed

I sabella had built an enviable career as a graphic designer. She had clients across industries, a steady stream of work, and a portfolio that spoke for itself. Clean, polished, and on-trend. Her designs appeared on billboards, app interfaces, and glossy packaging.

But over time, she began to feel disconnected from her work. It wasn't the pace or the deadlines. It was the purpose.

She found herself designing branding for fast fashion lines she didn't believe in, digital ads for products she'd never use, and campaigns that felt manipulative instead of meaningful. The work was good. It paid well. But it no longer reflected *her*.

One day, after finishing a sleek campaign for a product she couldn't even explain, Isabella looked at her portfolio and realized it was beautiful, but not honest. It didn't tell the story of who she was anymore.

So she did something few creatives do voluntarily: she closed her books.

Not for a sabbatical. Not to respond to a tragedy. But because her heart had moved on.

The *trade-off* was between professional momentum and the discomfort of creative misalignment.

The *benefit* was rediscovering the kind of work that lit her up—partnering with nonprofits, local artisans, and purpose-driven brands.

The *consequence* was starting over in many ways with smaller clients, slower growth, and explaining over and over why she walked away from "success."

But Isabella built a new portfolio. One that wasn't just beautiful, but deeply true.

### Reflection Questions

Have you ever looked at your accomplishments and realized they no longer reflect who you are? What would it take to start again, this time on your terms?

# The Line The Doctor Drew

D r. Harris had spent most of his career on the edge of a breakthrough. His team was closer than ever to developing a treatment that could potentially slow the progression of a devastating neurological disease.

But there was a condition: the next phase of the research required extensive animal testing. It was legal. It was standard. It was even expected.

But for Harris, it wasn't right.

He had entered the field to help people, yes, but also to do no harm where it could be avoided. The idea of contributing to pain, even in pursuit of a cure, began to keep him up at night. He reviewed the protocols again and again, hoping for an alternative. There wasn't one.

So he stepped away.

The *trade-off* was monumental. He gave up authorship on the published findings, a possible award nomination, and a place in the spotlight of medical innovation.

The *benefit* was maintaining his integrity and being able to look in the mirror knowing he didn't cross a line he couldn't live with.

The *consequence* was professional isolation. Some colleagues saw him as principled. Others labeled him difficult, even unrealistic. Future grant opportunities were harder to come by. Invitations to speak dwindled.

But Dr. Harris never wavered. He chose to believe that science and ethics weren't mutually exclusive—and that some lines, once crossed, can't be uncrossed.

### Reflection Questions

When your values and your work collide, which one do you follow? What are you willing to lose to hold the line?

# The Return To Normal

Elena had been a competitive gymnast since she was six years old. By sixteen, she was a national champion with Olympic potential. Her life revolved around practice, perfection, and pressure. Every hour was scheduled. Every calorie counted. Every fall felt like failure.

But after narrowly missing the cut for the Olympic trials, something shifted. Elena started asking questions no one in her world wanted to answer: *What comes after this? Who am I outside of the gym?*

She made the unthinkable decision to quit elite gymnastics during her final year of high school. Coaches were stunned. Teammates were confused. Her parents tried to hide their disappointment.

The *trade-off* was between chasing the dream she had trained for her whole life and discovering a life outside of the sport.

The *benefit* was reclaiming her identity, her health, and her time, experiencing normal teenage milestones for the first time.

The *consequence* was stepping away from something she once believed defined her, and enduring the grief, uncertainty, and guilt that followed.

But slowly, Elena found herself again, not through medals, but through meaning.

**Reflection Questions**

Have you ever walked away from something that once defined you? What did you discover about yourself on the other side?

# STORY 54  The Oven Light Stayed On

Eleanor spent most of her adult life managing numbers—quarterly reports, tax filings, payroll. She was good at it. Respected. Safe. But somewhere between audits and spreadsheets, she tucked away a vision: a bakery of her own. Not just to bake, but to create a place that felt warm and comforting, like her grandmother's kitchen.

She nearly pursued it once, back in her thirties. But then life happened. Mortgage, braces, college tuition. So, she told herself, "Someday."

Decades later, with her kids grown and retirement brochures piling up on the counter, Eleanor realized that *someday* was running out of calendar space.

She gave her notice. Sold her car. Rented a small commercial space and painted the walls herself. At sixty-one, she opened the doors to "Butter & Grace," her first bakery.

The *trade-off* wasn't abstract: she walked away from a stable income, financial predictability, and the professional identity she'd carried for over thirty years.

The *benefit* was deeply personal: the joy of watching regulars return for her lemon scones, the pride in building something of her own, and the satisfaction of honoring a promise she made to herself decades ago.

The *consequence* was humbling. It involved navigating a steep learning curve, feeling out of place at networking events full of twenty-something entrepreneurs, and the gnawing doubt of whether she'd started too late.

But every morning, when she flipped on the oven light and breathed in the smell of cinnamon and courage, she knew she'd made the right choice.

### Reflection Question

If you knew it wasn't too late to try—what would you dare to begin?

# 55 The Breaking Point

Hannah had always been praised for her calm under pressure. As a nurse in a trauma unit, she handled chaos with grace. Stabilizing patients, comforting families, training new staff. Her badge read *Charge Nurse,* but her job felt more like emotional triage.

Everyone assumed she was fine because she never flinched.

Even after a particularly devastating week with a teenager lost in a car accident and a mother who had coded in the middle of visiting hours, she showed up early, stayed late, and took on the hardest cases without complaint. She was the one people turned to when they were overwhelmed. The steady one. The strong one.

But inside, something was shifting.

One night, she stood in a supply closet, holding a patient's file, unable to remember what room they were in. Her hands were shaking. Her chest was tight. She felt like she couldn't breathe. No one saw it. She pulled herself together, finished her shift, and went home in silence.

That was the night she knew something had to change.

The *trade-off* had never been obvious: it wasn't between day and night, or rest and work—it was between appearing invincible and admitting she wasn't okay.

The *benefit* of stepping away for three months on medical leave wasn't just rest. It was reclaiming her sense of self, her joy in nursing, and the ability to feel again without crumbling.

The *consequence* was confronting a hard truth: that sometimes, in the act of caring for everyone else, she had forgotten how to care for herself.

Hannah didn't stop being a nurse. But she came back on her own terms, in a new department, with boundaries she never thought she'd be brave enough to set.

### Reflection Questions

What role are you praised for that depletes you? What would change if you gave yourself permission to step back?

# 56 The Gamer's Pivot

J ason had always been a strategist. As a rising star in the e-sports world, he spent hours analyzing gameplay, refining tactics, and climbing the global rankings. Sponsors had started calling. Streamers asked him to collaborate. His name was becoming known in elite gaming circles.

The biggest tournament of the year was six weeks away, and he was predicted to win it.

But one evening, after a long stream, Jason noticed something in the chat: *"Wish I could talk to someone like you. No one understands how isolating this feels."*

It stopped him cold.

Over the next few days, he noticed similar messages from young players who looked up to him, confessing to burnout, anxiety, and loneliness. He had once been that kid—playing through the night to escape his own struggles, finding identity in the leaderboard when life felt out of control.

And suddenly, the trophy didn't feel like the finish line anymore.

Jason withdrew from the tournament.

Instead, he launched a community-focused gaming mentorship program for teens. He started hosting mental health conversations on his stream. He partnered with therapists to embed wellness tools into popular games. He didn't need to be the best in the world. He just needed to make the gaming world better.

The *trade-off* was stepping away from global competition and personal accolades.

The *benefit* was using his platform for purpose, helping thousands of gamers feel seen, supported, and less alone.

The *consequence* was leaving behind the spotlight he had spent years chasing, but what he gained was something more lasting: meaning.

### Reflection Question
Have you ever redefined what success looks like in order to align your passion with a greater purpose?

# The New Politician's Campaign

Sienna had always been more of a listener than a talker. But when she saw her hometown struggling—underfunded schools, shuttered small businesses, sidewalks that hadn't been repaired in years—she felt something stir that couldn't be ignored.

At twenty-three, with no political experience and barely enough in her bank account to cover rent, she made a decision that turned heads: she was going to run for local office.

Campaigning meant long hours walking neighborhoods, attending community forums, and cold-calling local donors. To fund it, she worked three side gigs, shared a one-bedroom apartment with two roommates, and relied on gas money from friends. She missed family dinners, weddings, and even her cousin's graduation, all replaced by campaign events and volunteer meetings.

Some called her naïve. Others called her bold. But she kept showing up, with scuffed shoes and a stack of handwritten flyers.

The *trade-off* was personal and profound. She gave up financial stability, social connection, and the soft runway most of her peers were enjoying post-college.

The *benefit* was that she won the election and quickly passed a measure that expanded access to mental health resources in local schools.

The *consequence* was that her friendships shifted, her family wondered when they'd see her smile without stress behind it, and her body carried the weight of constant burnout.

But when a mother grabbed her hand at a town hall and said, "Because of what you did, my daughter is getting help," Sienna knew: this was her work.

### Reflection Question

How much would you sacrifice to help your community?

The Role She
Never Applied For

**P**riya wasn't asked to take over the family. It was
simply assumed.

As the eldest of four, she had always been the
"responsible one"—the scheduler, the go-between, the
fixer of forgotten forms and last-minute rides. Her parents
were still alive but emotionally distant, consumed with
work, tradition, and survival. They relied on Priya to hold
things together. She was twenty-one, but in practice, she'd
been parenting since fourteen.

When she graduated from college, everyone expected
her to stay close to help with her youngest brother's school
forms, manage the college applications for her sister, and
handle hospital visits for her grandfather. Grad school offers
came in, including one from a top school out of state. She
didn't even tell her family. It felt impossible.

Priya declined the offers and stayed home.

No dramatic event. No tragedy. Just the soft pressure of familial expectation wrapped in cultural duty. Her sacrifice wasn't loud. It was consistent and largely unseen.

The *trade-off* was between pursuing her vision for her future and fulfilling the role everyone expected her to play.

The *benefit* was preserving family stability and being the one everyone could count on.

The *consequence* was her dreams slowly fading under the weight of what others needed, and a gnawing question she carried alone: *What if I had left?*

Priya doesn't regret staying. But she often wonders how long she can keep holding everything before she lets herself become someone beyond the oldest child.

### Reflection Questions

What expectations have shaped your life that you never consciously agreed to? What would it look like to let them go?

STORY
59

# The Project
# He Didn't Plan

Greg had been a structural engineer for over forty years. Retirement was supposed to be simple. Fishing, golfing, maybe traveling with his wife. After decades of deadlines and city permits, he was ready for silence.

But a few weeks in, the silence became too loud.

One afternoon, while running errands, he walked past an old warehouse on the edge of town. A faded sign read highlighting it was the future site of a transition space for young adults. A group of volunteers stood nearby, staring at an incomplete foundation with blueprints flapping in the wind.

Curious, Greg stepped in and introduced himself. Within five minutes, he was asked if he could "take a quick look" at a problem with the framing. Five minutes turned into five months.

Greg hadn't planned on this. He didn't sign up to manage the rebuild, train volunteers, or deal with suppliers. He also hadn't expected the conversations with twenty-somethings navigating homelessness, or the way his precise, problem-solving brain could build more than just walls.

The *trade-off* wasn't just between personal leisure and community service; it was between a restful retreat from his past life and a surprising re-entry into purpose.

The *benefit* was rediscovering his value in a world that often overlooks older people, and forming friendships that transcended age.

The *consequence* was shelving his golf clubs and skipping lazy mornings, but what he built in return wasn't just a shelter. It was a sense of usefulness he didn't know he'd been missing.

## Reflection Question

How do you decide when to use your skills to give back instead of focusing solely on your personal enjoyment?

STORY
# 60 The Invisible Post

G ia wasn't in the military, but her life was ruled by its orders.

Her husband, a dedicated Marine, wore the uniform. Gia wore everything else. The moves, the paperwork, the goodbyes, the solo parenting stretches, the endless waiting. Every two to three years, the address changed. So did the schools, the neighbors, the doctor's office, and the license plates.

On paper, she was "dependable dependent." In reality, she was the anchor.

But what no one saw was the toll it took. She applied for dozens of jobs, only to be told she was "overqualified," "under committed," or simply not worth the training because she'd be gone again in two years. Her career became a patchwork of short contracts and roles that never quite fit.

The deeper cost, though, wasn't professional. It was personal. In every new place, Gia had to reinvent herself while making sure everyone else felt at home.

The *trade-off* was between building a self-directed life and holding steady for the one her spouse was called to live.

The *benefit* was the unshakable pride of being part of something bigger: a team, a mission, a family.

The *consequence* was a growing pain: that her own dreams had no rank, no medals, and no applause.

Eventually, Gia found her voice, not through a job title, but through advocacy. She began mentoring other military spouses, writing about the emotional labor behind the scenes, and reminding the world that service isn't always in uniform.

### Reflection Question
How do you maintain your identity when love or loyalty places you in someone else's shadow?

# 61 The Chef's Realization

Elliot had trained at the finest culinary schools and worked his way through elite restaurant kitchens in New York and Tokyo. When he was offered a coveted position at a Michelin-starred restaurant in Paris, it felt like the final step in a perfectly plated career.

The job promised everything: prestige, mentorship under a culinary icon, and a fast track to becoming a global name in fine dining.

But there was one catch.

The kitchen culture was brutal. Long hours. Toxic egos. Zero room for creativity. Elliot would be executing someone else's vision, someone else's sauces, someone else's story. He'd be climbing a ladder that didn't feel like his.

Around the same time, he visited his hometown and walked past the corner bakery where he got his first job washing pans. The owner, now nearing retirement, mentioned she was looking to sell.

And just like that, Elliot felt torn, not between obligation and ambition, but between *who he thought he was supposed to become and what actually felt true.*

He turned down Paris.

Instead, he bought the bakery.

He transformed it into a neighborhood bistro that served simple, soulful food, locally sourced, with recipes that carried stories, not just technique. No white tablecloths. No tasting menus. Just people connecting over plates.

The *trade-off* was walking away from prestige and fame to pursue something smaller and deeply personal.

The *benefit* was creative freedom, community connection, and falling in love with cooking all over again.

The *consequence* was letting go of a path that many dreamed of, but realizing he had never really wanted it in the first place.

Elliot didn't become a celebrity chef. But on most days, as he wiped flour from his apron and listened to the hum of conversation in his dining room, he knew he had made the right choice.

### Reflection Question

When the world offers you its definition of success, how do you know if it's truly your own?

# The Single Parent's Voyage

C armen didn't plan on raising two kids alone, but when her marriage ended abruptly, she didn't flinch. She restructured her life overnight: working the front desk at a medical clinic by day and cleaning offices after hours. Weekends were for laundry, budget planning, and cheering from the sidelines at soccer games and school plays, coffee in hand, sleep in short supply.

Her kids never missed a field trip or art class. Carmen made sure of it.

But somewhere along the way, Carmen's world shrank. She hadn't read a book for pleasure in years. Her piano sat untouched. She couldn't remember the last time she had a conversation that wasn't about homework, bills, or grocery lists. She told herself it was for a short time. *Just until they're older. Just until I can breathe.*

The *trade-off* was between her well-being and her children's future.

The *benefit* was watching her kids grow confident, capable, and resilient, knowing they had what she never did.

The *consequence* was heavy, stress-induced migraines, missed doctor appointments, and the ache of losing pieces of herself to the pace of survival.

Carmen never expected applause. But one night, as her daughter handed her a handmade birthday card that simply read, "*Thank you for everything you've given up so we can become who we are.*" She wept, for both the cost and the beauty of the voyage.

### Reflection Question

When was the last time you gave yourself permission to rest, even while carrying the weight of others?

# 63 The New Classroom

Alexandra was thriving in a top-tier suburban school. Her classroom was fully stocked, her colleagues were supportive, and her students arrived each day well-fed, well-prepared, and surrounded by family involvement. She had worked hard to get there, and on paper, it was the dream teaching job.

But something gnawed at her.

After volunteering one summer in a rural district, Alexandra couldn't stop thinking about the students there. Kids sharing torn textbooks, rotating teachers mid-year, and learning in overcrowded classrooms. She felt a tug she couldn't ignore.

When a job opened in that same rural district, she applied.

Accepting it meant leaving behind the life she had built: weekend brunches with friends, her favorite yoga studio, and her proximity to family. It also meant moving to a town where she was the outsider, adjusting to limited resources, and battling systems that had been broken long before she arrived.

The *trade-off* was between personal comfort and meaningful challenge.

The *benefit* was profound: Alexandra became a consistent force in her students' lives, helping several become the first in their families to graduate high school.

The *consequence* was long weekends spent alone, the ache of missing out on her old social circle, and a feeling of being indispensable in a town not yet sure how to welcome her.

But every time a student said, "*You believed in me when no one else did,*" Alexandra knew she had made the right kind of hard choice.

### Reflection Questions

Would you leave a life of comfort to serve where you're needed most? Why or why not?

# The Freelancer's Pick

Jordan was in demand. As a freelance designer, his clean style and sharp instincts had landed him bigger clients year after year. When a major agency approached him with a full-time offer as creative director with a six-figure salary and benefits, he didn't hesitate long.

It meant structure. Prestige. Security for his growing family.

What it didn't mean was flexibility.

Jordan's son had just turned three. His days were full of discovery and mischief, and Jordan had loved being around to see it. But now, meetings filled his calendar. Deadlines stacked up. Travel started creeping in.

He told himself it wouldn't be necessary forever. That he was building a better future.

The *trade-off* was clear. He chose momentum and financial growth over midday walks, bedtime stories, and unstructured afternoons.

The *benefit* was professional validation. His name was finally on award-winning campaigns. His LinkedIn inbox buzzed with recruiters.

The *consequence* came slowly. Missed milestones, evenings spent catching up on emails, a growing awareness that someone else was witnessing the firsts he used to treasure.

He didn't regret the decision. He believed in providing. But he also understood that while you can always chase more work, you can't replay a toddler's wonder.

One night, after putting in another twelve-hour day, he found a drawing his son made. Jordan's wife had written the caption: "*My favorite person is Daddy. He works a lot.*"

And for the first time in months, Jordan sat still.

---

**Reflection Question**

When providing for your family becomes your focus, how do you make sure you don't become a stranger to the life you're providing for?

# The Room Down The Hall

Sophia walked across the stage debt-free, degree in hand, résumé polished. While most of her classmates moved into starter apartments and joined the "real world," she made a different call. She moved back into her childhood bedroom.

It wasn't the plan she had imagined. Her posters were still on the wall. Her parents asked where she was going. Privacy was a memory. But Sophia ran the numbers, and her goal was clear: buy a home by twenty-six, no co-signer, no crushing debt.

She skipped spontaneous trips, shared her car with her younger brother, and learned to say no to happy hour because she was tracking every dollar. Friends teased her. Some envied her. A few distanced themselves.

The *trade-off* was her early twenties lived on someone else's terms. Curfews and missed independence.

The *benefit* was that at twenty-six, she held the keys to a condo in her name, with savings intact and no monthly rent draining her income.

The *consequence* was less visible: the ache of not having lived on her own during the years her friends were learning to burn toast, build IKEA furniture, and host awkward wine nights in overpriced apartments.

She gained security—but lost a little spontaneity along the way.

### Reflection Question

How do you weigh the benefits of delayed gratification against immediate satisfaction?

# 66 The Doctor's Sabbatical

D r. Jones had everything she thought she wanted: a bustling private practice, a packed calendar, glowing reviews, and a reputation as one of the best internal medicine doctors in the city.

But something was off.

She found herself exhausted, not just physically, but emotionally. Her days blurred together, filled with patient charts, insurance codes, and seven-minute appointments that barely scratched the surface of what people truly needed. The work had become transactional, the system relentless. She was healing others, but losing herself.

One evening, after realizing she had forgotten her own birthday, Dr. Jones paused. Instead of burning out completely, she made a radical choice: a six-month sabbatical, not to volunteer abroad, not to write a book, not even to reinvent her practice. Just to stop. To rest. To learn again what it meant to feel whole.

She enrolled in a wellness retreat not as a speaker, but as a guest. She took courses in nutrition and somatic therapy. She hiked without a Fitbit, cooked without a timer, and began to journal, not about patient outcomes, but about joy, silence, and breath.

The *trade-off* wasn't just income and client continuity. It was letting go of being constantly needed, admired, and defined by productivity.

The *benefit* was profound: a rediscovery of why she became a doctor in the first place—to witness, to hold space, to truly listen.

The *consequence* was that some patients moved on, the practice took a hit, and she returned to a world that had kept spinning without her. But she came back changed.

Dr. Jones restructured her practice to prioritize fewer patients, longer visits, and integrative care. She healed differently now. More fully. Including herself.

### Reflection Questions

When was the last time you paused not because you had to—but because you chose to? What did it give back to you?

# 67 The Artist's Exhibition

S amantha didn't paint for galleries. She painted because she had to. Because it was the one place in her life where she felt free and fully herself. Her small studio was lined with works she'd never shown anyone. One in particular, an abstract oil she titled *The Quiet After The Waves*, had always stayed with her. It held memories, loss, and a breakthrough she could never quite describe. It was her.

When a respected gallery offered her a solo exhibition, she was thrilled. But there was a catch: she needed funds for framing, venue costs, and promotion. Her savings wouldn't stretch far enough. A collector had once expressed interest in *The Quiet After The Waves*. The offer remained.

She sat with it for days.

Selling it would mean giving up something deeply personal. Her best piece, maybe forever. But it would also give her a shot. Exposure. Momentum. A career beyond commission work and weekend pop-ups.

The *trade-off* was sacrificing something that felt like an extension of herself to invest in the possibility of something bigger.

The *benefit* was undeniable. The exhibition was a success. She sold multiple pieces, landed two commissions, and finally felt seen.

The *consequence* was harder to name. A persistent sorrow every time she saw the blank space on the wall where that painting used to live.

She told herself, sometimes letting go is part of making space for what's next.

### Reflection Question

How do you decide when letting go of something precious is worth it for future opportunities?

# The Fields
# He Reimagined

L eo grew up under wide skies and dusty boots, working the same soil his great-grandfather had tilled nearly a century before. The farm had been passed down like a sacred promise, generation after generation, stitched into the identity of his family and the respect of the local community.

But Leo had other dreams.

In college, he fell in love with urban planning—systems thinking, sustainable development, smart cities. He dreamed of reshaping spaces that connected people, of designing green rooftops and walkable neighborhoods. His professors urged him to apply for a master's program. The city called to him.

But then his father's health declined. The paperwork for inheritance surfaced. The community whispered, "Leo will take it over, of course."

He nearly signed the papers out of obligation. But paused. What if this wasn't a *goodbye* to his dream, but a *reframe*?

Leo returned to the farm. But not as a carbon copy of his father.

He brought with him the mindset of a planner. He studied regenerative agriculture, installed solar panels, launched a local farm-to-table co-op, and turned a section of the land into a community garden with education programs for local schools.

The neighbors were skeptical at first. Then curious. Then inspired.

The *trade-off* wasn't between tradition and ambition. It was between following a familiar path and creating a new one.

The *benefit* was both preserving his family's heritage *and* evolving it into something sustainable and forward-looking.

The *consequence* was sacrificing the prestige of a big-city career. but what he built was rooted, real, and entirely his.

Leo didn't abandon legacy. He redefined it.

### Reflection Question

What if honoring your past doesn't mean repeating it, but reshaping it into something only you could have imagined?

# 69 The Unseen Victory

L isa was at her peak. Qualifying for the Boston Marathon, setting personal records, and finally attracting attention from major sponsors. Her name was beginning to appear in articles. She was the runner to watch.

But as her public momentum accelerated, something was unraveling behind the scenes.

Her younger sister, Michelle, had been diagnosed with a rare autoimmune disorder. The illness was unpredictable. Some days she was fine, some days she needed hospital visits. Lisa had always promised to be there for her. But now, training required full focus: twenty-mile runs, strict schedules, out-of-state races, and recovery protocols.

One morning, during a long run, Lisa's phone buzzed. Michelle had collapsed at school. Their parents couldn't get there quickly. Lisa was two hours away.

She finished the run. But the victory felt hollow.

That night, Lisa made a decision that would shock her sponsors and break her own heart: she stepped away from professional racing, not due to injury, but by choice.

The *trade-off* was between continuing the climb toward national recognition and being fully present for her sister during the most uncertain time of her life.

The *benefit* was deeper than medals: she became a constant in Michelle's recovery—her cheerleader, her late-night snack runner, her calm in the storm.

The *consequence* was the slow fading of a dream she had trained for since childhood as she watched from the sidelines.

But years later, when Michelle crossed her own finish line, healthy, joyful, pursuing her own career, Lisa knew she had still helped someone win.

### Reflection Question

Have you ever given up something you loved—not because you had to, but because someone else needed you more?

# The Company He Let Go

Alex had built the company from the ground up—garage to growth phase, pitch decks to product launch. Every milestone had his fingerprints on it. Investors trusted him. Employees rallied behind him. He wasn't just the CEO. He was the company.

But at some point, the version of himself that thrived in chaos began to unravel.

His sleep got shorter. His temper got shorter. His kids started referring to "Dad's office" as if it were a far-off country. And the spark he once had, curiosity, creativity, and courage, was being replaced by fatigue and a daily dread.

That's when he made the hardest call of his life: he stepped down.

He didn't sell. He didn't crash. He handed over the reins to his chief of staff. Someone he trusted. But it felt like walking away from a part of who he is.

The *trade-off* was more than just stepping out of the corner office; it was surrendering control over the thing he'd built from nothing.

The *benefit* was that his health improved, his relationships began to mend, and he started remembering what it felt like to be present.

The *consequence* lingered. He watched his company from the sidelines, cheering it on, while sometimes wondering if he'd just become a footnote in a success story he authored.

He ultimately redefined what "achievement" looked like when the applause faded, and the calendar cleared.

### Reflection Question

When leadership begins to cost you your peace, how do you know it's time to let go?

## STORY 71 The Volunteer Firefighter

I n Ben's small town, sirens meant one thing. Someone needed help. And more often than not, Ben answered the call.

As a volunteer firefighter, he wasn't paid. He wasn't chasing glory. He simply believed that showing up mattered.

That meant leaving in the middle of dinner. He missed his daughter's choir performance. Skipped movie nights with his wife. At times, his presence at home is nonexistent.

Neighbors called him a hero. But his kids sometimes called him late. His wife, endlessly supportive, flinched every time his phone lit up during a birthday or holiday.

The *trade-off* was clear: personal moments exchanged for service, consistency sacrificed for responsibility.

The *benefit* was tangible: lives saved, homes protected, a deep-rooted sense of purpose.

The *consequence* was harder to talk about. A lingering guilt that while he showed up for strangers, his family sometimes got the leftovers.

Ben believed in answering the call. But he also began learning to set boundaries. Passing on some calls, scheduling family days with his phone powered down, trusting others on the team to carry the load.

Because being there for your community matters. But so does being home when the candles are lit.

### Reflection Question

When your duty to others pulls you away from those you love most, how do you know when to say yes and when to stay?

# 72 The Actor's Audition

harlotte had always been the reliable one. In her small hometown, she led school plays, worked double shifts at the coffee shop, and helped care for her younger brother. Everyone said she was talented, but no one expected her to leave.

Until one night, she saw a casting call for a film with an up-and-coming director. It was in Los Angeles, just three days away. The audition was in person only. Her rent was due the following week. She had $500 in her account.

Charlotte didn't hesitate.

She bought the plane ticket, packed two outfits, and left a note for her roommates: "*Trust me. I have to try.*"

The audition didn't lead to the role. But something else happened. A casting assistant slipped her a card afterward, saying, "*You have something. Stay in touch.*"

That card led to a series of callbacks. Eventually, a recurring role on a streaming series.

The *trade-off* wasn't just financial, it was leaving behind the identity others expected of her: dependable, predictable, selfless.

The *benefit* was stepping fully into who she was meant to become—a bold, creative person who was willing to take risks.

The *consequence* was weeks of living off instant noodles, missed rent, and phone calls from family wondering if she was okay. But the reward wasn't just work. It was proving to herself that she could choose *herself.*

### Reflection Question

What would you risk financially, emotionally, or socially, to step into the version of yourself you've only imagined?

# 73 The Mentor's Time

Diego was a respected engineer with a wall of patents and a steady career in advanced robotics. He was also private, especially about his past.

When asked to lead a Saturday STEM program for high school students in underserved neighborhoods, he initially declined. He wasn't a teacher. He wasn't "good with kids." But when a colleague called in a favor, he reluctantly agreed to try it—just once.

That first session was chaos: laughter, loud music, late arrivals. But in the back row sat Mateo, a sixteen-year-old who asked a single question that stopped Diego in his tracks: *"You ever grow up with people telling you this stuff wasn't for you?"*

Diego had. He just hadn't said it out loud in twenty years.

Each Saturday, Diego showed up—not just with schematics and soldering kits, but eventually, with pieces of his story. He talked about growing up in a blue-collar family, being the only Latino student in his engineering program, and the shame he once felt for dreaming too big.

The *trade-off* wasn't just free time. It was emotional safety. He gave up the comfort of compartmentalization to show up more fully, more vulnerably.

The *benefit* wasn't just seeing students like Mateo light up with confidence. It was reconnecting with the younger version of himself he'd tried to forget.

The *consequence* was a slow, sometimes painful unraveling of the narrative he had built to succeed, but what took its place was far more powerful: authenticity.

Diego didn't just teach robotics. He taught possibility, and, for the first time, he believed in his own again.

### Reflection Question

When was the last time you helped someone else— and in doing so, unlocked something in yourself?

# 74 The Geographic Leap

L eila left everything she knew. Her language, her traditions, her late-night talks with her sister on the rooftop, to board a one-way flight to a country where she knew no one.

She came for a master's degree. A scholarship gave her access. Ambition gave her courage. But no one told her how lonely ambition can feel when you're surrounded by a new alphabet, new customs, and a silence that stretches between phone calls home across time zones.

She celebrated her birthday alone that first year, eating store-bought cake in her room while pretending it didn't matter. Her mom called, and they both cried.

The *trade-off* was unmistakable: she exchanged her cultural identity, comfort, and constant support for uncertainty, adaptation, and starting over from scratch.

The *benefit* came first with passing exams, then a coveted internship, then an offer to stay and work in her new country.

The *consequence* was harder to define: homesickness that never fully left, family milestones missed, and the feeling of being a visitor in both her new world and the old one when she returned.

But she carried on because she was building not just a new life, but a bridge. One that others in her family would one day walk across.

### Reflection Question

How do you manage the emotional toll of pursuing opportunities far from home?

STORY
## 75 The Parent's Farewell

For most of her son Jack's childhood, Eleanor had been his everything. She packed the lunches, cheered from the bleachers, and helped build volcanoes for science fairs. They had inside jokes. Shared playlists. Friday pizza nights.

Then came adolescence.

Jack didn't pull away with defiance, just silence. One-word answers. Closed doors. Headphones on. The kind of distance that stings more than slamming doors or shouted arguments. At first, Eleanor tried harder. She showed up to everything. Left notes. Made his favorite meals.

Nothing seemed to reach him.

One evening, she stood outside his bedroom, holding a tray of warm cookies, and heard him laughing—not with her, but with friends through his headset. It hit her harder than she expected.

She turned back, set the tray down on the kitchen counter, and sat alone with the ache.

The *trade-off* wasn't a dramatic goodbye. It was surrendering her role as center of his universe without a clear invitation into the next chapter.

The *benefit* was giving Jack the space he needed to grow into himself, unpressured by her presence.

The *consequence* was grief: mourning the closeness that once was, without resentment, but with a deep, persistent longing.

Eleanor didn't push. She waited. And one day, after a long silence, Jack knocked on *her* door and asked, "Hey, want to help me pick colleges?"

She smiled—not because she was needed again, but because she had trusted the space between them would one day shrink.

### Reflection Question

How do you honor love when it no longer looks like closeness, and trust that letting go doesn't mean losing?

# The Soldier's Homecoming

For over twenty years, Juan had worn the same uniform, woken to the same cadence, and followed the same code. He had been deployed, decorated, and depended on. The military hadn't just shaped him. It *was* him.

So when retirement came, everyone expected him to relax. He moved into a quiet neighborhood. Bought a dog. Went fishing. People thanked him for his service at the grocery store. But inside, Juan felt hollow.

He missed structure. Missed purpose. Missed *belonging*.

One afternoon, he tried to volunteer at a local veteran support group. But the stories they shared weren't about combat. They were about addiction, divorce, and panic attacks in parking lots. Juan nodded, but said little. He didn't know how to be useful if he wasn't in control.

The truth hit hard: he didn't know who he was without the mission.

And so, his sacrifice began, not for his country, but for himself.

Juan gave up the identity that had once defined him. He stopped introducing himself as "Sergeant." He sought therapy. He joined a community art class and took up woodworking, sitting among civilians who didn't ask him about the war. He began writing poetry, never to publish, just to process.

The *trade-off* was significant. He let go of the persona that had made him feel strong, respected, and needed.

The *benefit* was something deeper. He discovered he could be whole without a uniform.

The *consequence* was the grief of shedding a skin he'd worn for decades, but what emerged was someone softer, more human, and worthy.

### Reflection Question

What identities have you outgrown, and what might open up if you allowed yourself to step into who you're becoming?

# The Student's Late Start

S heri watched her friends pack up for college while she unpacked boxes at the retail job she'd taken after graduation. Not because she lacked ambition, but because she had two younger siblings and parents struggling to stay afloat.

Instead of moving into a dorm, she moved into the night shift. Saving money for books she'd never read, tuition she wouldn't use, at least not yet.

She told herself that her time would come.

And it did! Two years later, after her siblings were squared away with what they needed, Sheri enrolled in community college with a modest savings account and a maturity her classmates didn't yet carry.

She didn't resent the delay. But she did feel its weight. Socially out of sync, starting when others were finishing, explaining why she was "older than the rest of the cohort." Some days it felt like falling behind—other days, like leading.

The *trade-off* was her own timeline—postponed dreams, missed dorm life, and the feeling of starting late.

The *benefit* was walking across her graduation stage debt-free, with no guilt, and knowing she helped open doors for her siblings before unlocking her own.

The *consequence* was subtle: she started her career later, built her network more slowly, and sometimes wondered how different things could have been.

But every time her sister texted about a college paper or her brother called for advice, she knew—it was never really a delay. It was a gift.

### Reflection Questions

Have you ever put your life on hold for someone else? What did you learn about yourself in the waiting?

# The Entrepreneur's Loss

Jackson wasn't reckless. He didn't gamble. He ran projections. Built models. Met with mentors. But when it came time to fund his start-up, a platform he believed could disrupt an outdated industry, traditional investors didn't bite.

So he bet on himself.

He sold his house. The home where he'd raised his kids. The place that held a decade of memories. He moved into a rental on the edge of town and put every dollar into the business.

At first, things looked promising. Momentum. Buzz. Clients. But then a major contract fell through. A key developer quit. The market shifted. And just like that, the dream unraveled.

The *trade-off* was painful and permanent: he gave up financial stability, comfort, and the life he'd carefully built.

The *benefit* didn't show up right away. But over time, the failure became fuel. He learned about grit, blind spots, resilience, and how to build smarter next time.

The *consequence* was heavy: his credit took a hit. His pride took a bigger one. And even when his next venture succeeded, the echo of that first loss stayed with him.

He wouldn't take it back because failure didn't break him. It broke open what he needed to grow.

### Reflection Question

What would you risk—truly risk—to build something you believe in?

## STORY 79

# The Saturdays She Gave Away

Carla didn't clock out at 3:15 p.m.

Her classroom door stayed open long after the final bell. First for a student struggling with algebra, then for another who needed a silent place to finish an essay.

But it didn't stop there.

Every Saturday morning, while her neighbors sipped coffee or went to yoga, Carla opened her living room to students who had fallen behind. No charge. No fanfare. Just time, patience, and an old whiteboard propped against her bookcase.

She thought that this was just until midterms, just until the next report cards.

But weeks became months, and rest became a luxury she forgot how to prioritize.

The *trade-off* was her own downtime. Sleep, errands, brunches with friends, all replaced by red pens and lesson plans.

The *benefit* was watching her students slowly gain confidence, watching grades rise, and receiving thank-you notes from parents who didn't know what else to say.

The *consequence* crept in slowly: fatigue that never lifted, evenings where she couldn't keep her eyes open past 8 p.m., and the realization that even purpose needs boundaries.

Eventually, Carla scaled back. Not because she cared less, but because she finally understood that burning out helps no one, not even the students you care most about.

### Reflection Question

When your work is driven by purpose, how do you know when it's time to rest—and give something back to yourself?

# The Raise
# He Declined

Hector was in his seventh year as CEO of a mid-sized manufacturing firm. The company had grown steadily. Nothing flashy, but solid margins, stable jobs, and a workforce that trusted him. He believed in long games, not flashy headlines.

When the board reviewed performance that year, they recommended a generous pay raise and an executive bonus pool. Profits were up, competitors were downsizing, and on paper, Hector had earned every penny.

But what the spreadsheets didn't show was the aging machinery in Plant 3. Or the increased turnover in the warehouse. Or the rising health insurance premiums employees were shouldering.

Hector made a decision he didn't announce.

He declined the raise.

Instead, he asked that the funds be redirected to modernize outdated equipment and expand the employee wellness program, moves that would never make headlines but would ripple throughout the company in impactful ways.

The *trade-off* was personal: he gave up well-earned financial gains, delayed his own compensation growth, and risked pushback from peers who believed he was "setting a dangerous precedent."

The *benefit* was a stronger, safer company and a culture that felt cared for. Productivity went up. So did retention.

The *consequence* was that while others in his network celebrated their rising net worth, Hector wondered if he'd made too quiet a choice. There were no awards. No write-ups. Just steadiness.

But for him, that was enough.

### Reflection Question

When no one is watching, what choices do you make that define who you really are as a leader?

# The Court He Returned To

After years of buzzer beaters, packed arenas, and post-game interviews, Jake had finally retired from professional basketball. For the first time in decades, his days were his own. He planned to travel. To sleep in. To finally take up the trumpet.

Then a call came from the local high school.

They were looking for a coach. Not just someone to run drills, but someone the players would respect. Someone who'd *been there*.

Jake hesitated. He'd spent his whole life around the game. Didn't he deserve a break?

But something pulled at him. Maybe it was the memory of his first coach, or maybe it was the idea of giving these kids a head start he never had. Either way, two weeks later, he was on the sidelines again, clipboard in hand.

The *trade-off* was that he gave up leisure, hobbies, and hard-won freedom for crowded gyms, long bus rides, and late-night phone calls from anxious parents.

The *benefit* was immeasurable: watching young athletes grow in confidence, discipline, and heart and helping them win not just games, but belief in themselves.

The *consequence* was personal. His retirement didn't look like what he'd imagined. He missed some of the rest he'd earned. But he discovered a purpose that went beyond the scoreboard.

Jake didn't return to the court for nostalgia. He returned to pass the torch.

### Reflection Question

How do you balance personal passions with opportunities to mentor others?

# 82 The Lab She Chose

D r. Elena was offered what many would consider a dream job—leading a cutting-edge research division at a global biotech firm with a salary three times her current pay. It came with a team, a generous budget, and stock options.

She almost said yes.

But there was a catch. The work, while important, would be proprietary, locked behind NDAs. It wouldn't belong to the public. And it wouldn't allow her to continue her independent research on a rare degenerative disease, something she'd been chipping away at for the past five years.

Her project had no guaranteed payoff, no fast results, and no big backers. But Elena believed it could lead to something revolutionary, eventually.

She stayed in academia.

The *trade-off* was steep: she gave up financial security, recognition, and the platform that came with corporate prestige.

The *benefit* was freedom, intellectual autonomy, the ability to publish openly, and the hope that her work could one day change the trajectory of an overlooked disease.

The *consequence* was living on a modest university salary while watching peers accelerate ahead, and enduring questions from colleagues who didn't understand why she'd "turn down something that big."

But in the calm of her lab, late at night, when the data started to show promise, Dr. Elena didn't need validation. She knew she was exactly where she needed to be.

### Reflection Question

When the path to purpose is slower and harder, how do you remind yourself it's still the right one?

# The Hours She Gave Away

By day, Samantha's apartment was full of life. Her twin daughters are building pillow forts, reading aloud, and asking endless questions. She packed lunches, helped with homework, and snuck in hugs between chores. It was the part of her life that people saw.

What they didn't see was the second half.

At 9:30 p.m., as the neighborhood dimmed, Samantha clocked in at a local packaging plant. The machines were loud. The work was repetitive. Most of her coworkers were twice her age or didn't speak much English. There were no birthday cakes in the break room, no stories over coffee—just tired bodies moving through a night that never seemed to end.

Samantha chose this shift so her girls didn't have to attend daycare during the day and not grow up in constant transition. It was a schedule that worked for everyone except her.

She missed family dinners, adult friendships, and daylight. She slept in fragments. No one asked her to volunteer at school because they assumed she couldn't. They were right.

The *trade-off* wasn't just sleep. It was the slow erosion of her social life, self-expression, and sense of being part of a community.

The *benefit* was consistency for her kids. Meals on the table, school events attended, and the feeling that someone was always there.

The *consequence* was invisibility. While she gave everything to hold the days together, her nights disappeared into the background of a life she was too tired to live fully.

But Samantha never forgot why she did it. And when her daughters, years later, asked her how she made it all work, she smiled and said, "I gave up the hours that no one else saw, so you could live the ones that mattered."

### Reflection Question

How do you manage sacrifices when they feel essential for your family's well-being?

The Environmentalist's Pledge

Connor had always been passionate about the environment. But passion wasn't enough—not for him. He wanted his life to reflect his convictions, even if it meant discomfort.

He didn't just go car-free. He stopped flying. He boycotted fast fashion, avoided plastic, composted religiously, and limited screen time to conserve energy. At first, it felt empowering. He was walking the talk.

Then came the harder part.

He began turning down trips with friends. Dinners at restaurants that didn't source locally. Holidays with family that required cross-country flights. Invitations slowed. Conversations got awkward. People rolled their eyes and said, "*Come on, one flight won't kill the planet.*"

Connor stuck to his values. But he noticed something unexpected: the more he committed to his cause, the more isolated he felt from the people he loved.

The *trade-off* wasn't just convenience—it was belonging.

The *benefit* was moral clarity, the peace of living in full alignment with what he believed.

The *consequence* was loneliness. A life lived on the ethical high ground, but sometimes without company.

When he spoke to classrooms about sustainability or helped neighbors build their first garden beds, Connor saw flickers of connection. He knew the change he was fighting for started slowly, one decision, one person, one uncomfortable conversation at a time.

### Reflection Question

How far are you willing to go to live in alignment with your principles?

# 85 The Redirection

Alice was a rising star in a boutique design firm. She had just landed her first solo campaign with a global brand and was on track for an art director role by year's end. Life was moving fast, and she liked it that way.

Then her dad, recently widowed and increasingly forgetful, began to slip.

It wasn't a dramatic collapse or crisis. It was slower— missed appointments, spoiled groceries, confusion over bills. Living two states away, Alice tried to manage from a distance. But every phone call left her unsettled. Every visit revealed new gaps.

One night, after realizing he had driven to the store and forgotten why, she made a radical decision: she moved home.

She didn't frame it as quitting her career. She called it "pivoting," but she knew what it meant. She took on part-time freelance work and became her father's steady presence: scheduling appointments, simplifying his routine, reintroducing joy where confusion had crept in.

The *trade-off* was between professional acceleration and emotional caregiving.

The *benefit* was offering her father safety, dignity, and connection during a vulnerable stage of life.

The *consequence* was stepping off a creative career track she had fought hard to build, and feeling, at times, forgotten by the professional world she once thrived in.

But Alice discovered something new. A deeper form of design, reworking the rhythm of a life with compassion and care.

### Reflection Question

How do you balance your own ambitions with the needs of loved ones?

# STORY 86
# The Whiteboard In The Basement

After four decades as an engineer, Liam thought retirement would feel like a reward. No meetings. No deadlines. Plenty of time for fishing, travel, and long breakfasts.

But within six months, something felt off. The silence didn't soothe, it echoed.

One afternoon, while organizing his garage, Liam stumbled on an old whiteboard. It sparked a memory of mentoring interns, drawing equations in the margins of blueprints. He missed *teaching*.

A week later, he walked into a local nonprofit offering free tutoring for underserved kids. They were short-staffed. Math scores were low. Liam signed up for two hours a week.

It quickly turned into five. Then ten.

He gave up morning golf. Cut back on weekend trips. His calendar filled with lesson plans and volunteer coordination. He even started hosting Saturday study sessions in his basement for kids prepping for college entrance exams.

The *trade-off* wasn't glamorous; leisure gave way to long division. Retirement dreams gave way to donated snacks and dry-erase markers.

The *benefit* was watching kids, some who hated math, light up when they *got it*. Watching confidence grow where self-doubt once sat.

The *consequence* was that Liam's "golden years" looked nothing like the brochures. He was busier than ever. Tired, yes, but a different kind of fulfilled.

Liam didn't retire *from* something. He'd just retired *into* something else.

### Reflection Questions

When your time becomes fully your own, what will you choose to do with it? Who might benefit from your second chapter?

# 87 The Activist's Mission

Maya had advanced fast. By thirty-five, she had the corner office, a generous salary, stock options, and her name on the shortlist for VP. Her parents beamed with pride. Her LinkedIn inbox never sat empty.

But something didn't sit right.

Every time she walked past the rows of luxury condos near her office, she noticed the growing encampment on the other side of the street. She started volunteering at a local shelter after hours, just a couple of weekends. Then weekday evenings. Then, eventually, skipping work altogether to attend city council meetings on zoning laws and tenant rights.

The shift wasn't impulsive, but it felt inevitable.

She resigned.

Maya traded tailored blazers for protest tees. Her new "office" was a folding chair in a shared basement workspace. She organized rallies, wrote policy briefs, and helped draft legislation aimed at protecting renters and closing housing loopholes.

The *trade-off* was massive. Financial stability, career prestige, and the comfort of structure all replaced by risk, public scrutiny, and constant fundraising.

The *benefit* was profound. She helped pass tenant protection laws in three districts, kept vulnerable families from being evicted, and gave voice to stories long ignored.

The *consequence* was felt daily. Scraping by financially, strained friendships with former colleagues, and nights spent wondering whether this version of her life would ever feel "secure" again.

And yes, she stayed.

Because sometimes, fulfillment doesn't come with a title, but with impact.

### Reflection Question

What does purpose look like when it doesn't come with a paycheck?

STORY

## 88 The Teacher's Stand

J essica had spent over a decade in the same school. She had handmade posters, books with dog-eared pages, and students who returned just to say thank you. She wasn't just a teacher; she was a fixture in the community.

But things changed.

A new school board took over, and with it came rigid scripts, banned books, and a demand to "stick to curriculum, not conversation." Suddenly, discussions about history had to be sanitized. Social issues were off-limits. Even the novels she once used to spark empathy were pulled from her shelves.

At first, she tried to stay quiet and adapt. She needed the job. Her students needed her. But every time she skipped over something real to meet a mandate, it chipped away at her.

One morning, after a particularly tense meeting where a student project was shut down for being "too political,"

Jessica sat at her desk and stared at her lesson plan. It no longer felt like hers.

So she packed her things and resigned.

The *trade-off* wasn't location or income. It was between staying in a system that silenced her or stepping into uncertainty to preserve her values.

The *benefit* was reclaiming her voice and self-respect. She began tutoring, creating online content for progressive educators, and speaking publicly about censorship in classrooms.

The *consequence* was leaving behind a role she loved, and the daily connection to students she once inspired.

Jessica knew: the greatest lesson she could teach was the one she chose to live.

### Reflection Question

When do you choose to leave a role you love—because staying would mean losing a part of yourself?

# STORY 89 The Entrepreneur's Restart

Victor had done what most dream of. He built a successful startup from scratch, scaled it, sold it, and walked away with a comfortable fortune. The kind of exit that earns headlines, investor applause, and freedom.

But something was missing.

During the early days of his company, Victor hosted coding workshops for local high school students on weekends. A few kids had gone on to major in computer science. One even emailed years later to say the workshop "changed everything."

That stuck with him.

So instead of retiring or launching another company, Victor used the capital from his exit to start something with a different kind of return: a nonprofit teaching coding to under-resourced communities.

The *trade-off* was jarring. He gave up wealth accumulation, industry prestige, and the comfort of a seasoned executive team for the unpredictability of nonprofit fundraising, bureaucratic red tape, and starting from scratch—again.

The *benefit* was purpose, plain and simple. Watching a student write their first lines of code, land an internship, or get accepted into college. That payoff was unlike anything he'd built before.

The *consequence* was humbling. The pace was slower. The wins were fewer. There were days the old life looked easier. But Victor no longer measured success by IPOs or scale. He measured it in lives changed, one keyboard at a time.

### Reflection Question

How do you weigh personal success against the opportunity to uplift others?

# 90  The Final Sprint

Amira was at the top of her game. Team captain, international sponsorships, and just one match away from leading her team to their first-ever championship title. It was the culmination of years of early mornings, missed holidays, and pushing her body beyond its limits.

In the semifinals, she felt the pop.

The medical team confirmed it: a partial ligament tear. One more game, and she risked turning it into a full rupture, an injury that could end her career for good.

Her coaches gave her the option: sit it out and start rehab immediately, or play and potentially sacrifice everything she'd built.

The locker room was silent when she entered on game day.

She played.

Every sprint sent pain through her leg. Every cut and pivot felt like rolling the dice. But she scored the opening goal, and her presence kept her team steady under pressure. They won in overtime.

The *trade-off* was excruciatingly clear. She gave up her long-term health and future seasons for one last moment of glory.

The *benefit* was that she delivered a championship for her team, cemented her legacy, and walked (or limped) off the field as a hero.

The *consequence* was immediate. Surgery, a grueling recovery, and the realization that her professional playing days were over, sooner than they had to be.

Amira never regretted giving everything she had. But in some moments, she sometimes wondered what might've been if she'd said "not this time."

### Reflection Question
How do you decide when short-term gains are worth long-term risks?

# The Parents' Education

Henry and Sheila lived in a tight-knit suburban neighborhood where achievement was the currency of conversation. Every backyard barbecue buzzed with talk of honor rolls, AP classes, and early college acceptances. Their son, Caleb, didn't fit that mold.

He was bright, creative, curious, and endlessly kind, but he struggled in structured classroom settings. Diagnosed with sensory processing disorder and anxiety, Caleb often came home exhausted, withdrawn, or in tears. The traditional school system didn't know what to do with him. Neither did most of their friends.

When the school suggested a part-time special education program across town, the decision became a reality.

Sheila proposed a different path: homeschooling.

It wasn't just about income, though they'd lose one. It wasn't just about time, though it would consume hers. It was about stepping away from the rhythm of their community, from PTA meetings and science fairs, and into a world where Caleb's needs, not others' expectations, came first.

The *trade-off* was identity. They let go of what was familiar, comfortable, and socially accepted.

The *benefit* was meaningful. Caleb began to flourish, reading again for joy, building projects from scratch, and opening up.

The *consequence* was whispered judgments, fewer playdate invitations, and a lingering sense that they no longer fully belonged at the neighborhood table.

But when Caleb proudly presented a project he had built from concept to completion, a solar-powered model car he designed on his own, Sheila and Henry knew: they had given up belonging to one world in order to help their child thrive in his own.

### Reflection Question

When others question your path, how do you stay grounded in the conviction that you're doing what's right for your family?

## STORY 92 The Trip He Took Without Leaving

Antonio had always dreamed of disappearing for a year. Just him, a backpack, and the open road. He had the map marked, the gear packed, the notice given at work. A world trip: Southeast Asia and Eastern Europe. He was finally ready to live the adventure he'd been planning since college.

But a week before his departure, something unexpected happened.

At an open mic night, Antonio shared a short story he had written, something personal, vulnerable, and completely unlike the travel photos he usually posted online. To his surprise, the room fell silent, then erupted in applause. A publisher in the crowd approached him afterward: *"If you have more, I'd love to see it."*

He did have more. Boxes of handwritten stories and essays no one had ever read.

Antonio now faced a different kind of journey.

He canceled the trip.

Not to care for someone else. Not because he had to. But because, for the first time, he realized the story he truly needed to explore wasn't out there. It was inside him. He stayed home, rented a small studio apartment, and wrote.

The *trade-off* was between external adventure and internal excavation.

The *benefit* was rediscovering a long-buried calling and finally pursuing it with seriousness.

The *consequence* was missing the thrill of planes and new cities, but he unearthed something far richer: his voice.

When he finally traveled a year later, it was for a book tour.

### Reflection Question

What dream are you carrying that might only come alive if you pause another one?

STORY
93
# The Client No One Wanted

Johanna was a high-profile attorney known for corporate litigation. Her name appeared in industry journals, and her clients were powerful, well-funded, and nearly always on the winning side.

Then came the file no one wanted to touch.

It was a civil rights case involving a wrongfully accused teenager from a low-income neighborhood. The evidence was flawed, the media coverage harsh, and the case had become a political flashpoint. Johanna wasn't even on the shortlist of attorneys to review it, but something in her gut told her to read the case anyway.

The deeper she went, the harder it became to look away.

Taking it on meant turning down a lucrative client. It also meant alienating partners at her firm, some of whom subtly warned her: "*This isn't worth the heat.*"

She took the case anyway.

The *trade-off* was more than financial. It was risking her credibility in elite circles and fraying long-standing professional relationships.

The *benefit* was helping an innocent teen get his life back and restoring faith in a system that had nearly failed him.

The *consequence* was steep. Her promotion was tabled, two clients pulled their accounts, and whispers of her being "too emotional" followed her into boardrooms.

But Johanna slept better. She knew that justice isn't just a career. It's a compass.

### Reflection Question

When doing the right thing comes with a personal cost, what helps you stay grounded in your decision?

# The Shot She Didn't Take

L ila had spent years building her reputation as a premier wildlife photographer. Her images had been featured in glossy magazines and high-profile exhibits. She had a gift, not just for capturing rare animals, but for making people feel something when they looked at her work.

While photographing in a remote rainforest, Lila encountered a nest of one of the world's rarest birds. So rare, in fact, that its exact nesting location was unknown even to conservationists. The lighting was perfect. The composition sublime. She raised her lens.

And froze.

Lila knew that once this image went public, even with good intentions, it could bring researchers, influencers, and eco-tourists. People who might unknowingly threaten the fragile habitat. The bird's survival depended on secrecy.

She lowered her camera.

The *trade-off* was immense: passing up a career-defining photo to protect the very subject she loved.

The *benefit* was preserving the integrity of the environment and the safety of the species.

The *consequence* was no cover photo, no accolades, no viral moment, but she walked away knowing the bird had a better chance of flying again.

Sometimes the most powerful image is the one you choose not to share.

### Reflection Questions

When has doing the right thing meant stepping out of the spotlight? How did it change the way you define success?

# STORY 95
## The Journalist's Relocation

When the offer came to cover a developing crisis overseas, Evan knew what it meant. He'd be swapping his small apartment and morning coffee walks for checkpoints, military escorts, and the sound of gunfire in the distance.

Friends told him to turn it down. "It's not worth it," they said. But Evan believed some stories *had* to be told, especially the ones that others avoided.

In the conflict zone, comfort became a memory. Nights were spent in shelters, his few possessions crammed into a single backpack. Every day carried the calculus of risk. Choosing which roads to travel, which interviews to take, and when to move quickly if a situation turns.

The *trade-off* was sharp. Personal safety, predictable routines, and time with loved ones were replaced by danger, uncertainty, and constant vigilance.

The *benefit* was tangible and lasting. His reporting exposed corruption, gave displaced families a platform, and helped aid groups target critical needs.

The *consequence* was harder to carry. Persistent anxiety, sleepless nights, and the knowledge that the line between observer and casualty can be razor-thin.

Evan never pretended the decision was easy. But he couldn't walk away knowing his absence might leave the truth untold.

### Reflection Question

How do you determine when the risk is worth the story?

# 96 The Field She Chose

D r. Angela knew her work came with a cost the day she boarded a bush plane into the heart of the rainforest. Her mission was to study a critically endangered species found only in this remote corner of the world. A project with the potential to shape conservation policy for decades.

She expected the long days, the endless data sheets, and the patience it would take to earn the trust of the wildlife she observed. What she hadn't fully anticipated was the loneliness. No evening calls with friends. No spontaneous weekend visits to see family. Birthdays and holidays passed in spotty satellite messages and photos arriving weeks late by mail drop.

The *trade-off* was a deep connection with loved ones exchanged for the privilege of living immersed in her subject, miles from the nearest paved road.

The *benefit* was that her findings helped secure new protections for the species and its habitat, influencing both policy and public awareness.

The *consequence* was returning to civilization and realizing she was now a guest in the lives of people she loved, catching up on years she'd missed.

Dr. Angela never regretted her commitment. But she learned that even when you dedicate your life to saving something, it's worth asking what parts of your own life you're willing to let go.

### Reflection Question

When the pursuit of your passion takes you far from the people you love, how do you decide how far is too far?

# 97 The Last Companion

**P**aul had volunteered at the animal shelter for years, walking dogs, cleaning cages, helping with adoption events. He had seen hundreds of animals come and go—but one stayed.

Her name was Daisy. A fourteen-year-old mutt with cloudy eyes, stiff joints, and a heart condition. Everyone loved her, but no one adopted her. "Too old," they said. "Too hard to lose."

Paul visited her every day. She'd rest her chin on his knee and close her eyes like she belonged nowhere else.

He knew the risk. The vet said she might have a year, maybe less.

Paul signed the papers.

The *trade-off* wasn't just travel or finances. It was emotional: choosing to open his heart to inevitable heartbreak.

The *benefit* was emotional. Daisy spent her final months loved, safe, warm, and never alone.

The *consequence* was exactly what he feared: she passed away nine months later. The grief was sharp, but the regret? Nonexistent.

Paul didn't adopt Daisy to save her. He adopted her so she wouldn't die waiting for someone to try.

### Reflection Question

Would you be willing to love something fully, even if you knew from the start it would break your heart?

# The Inventor's Obsession

Leo believed the world needed a better answer to the energy crisis, and he was certain he could find it. What began as late-night tinkering in his garage evolved into a full-scale mission. He left his consulting job, sold off investments, and funneled everything (money, time, and focus) into developing a sustainable energy solution.

For years, the project consumed him. Dinner conversations drifted into monologues about prototypes and testing results. Vacations were postponed. Weekends disappeared into the workshop. He told himself the sacrifices were worth it, that the breakthrough would come any day.

And eventually, it did. His design passed safety testing and attracted interest from environmental organizations. The innovation had the potential to transform entire communities.

The *trade-off* involved chasing the dream of a cleaner future, he gave up years of everyday moments with his family, including school plays, weekend hikes, even relaxing evenings on the porch.

The *benefit* was tangible. A viable clean energy solution that could outlast him and make a measurable difference in the fight against climate change.

The *consequence* was harder to measure. Strained relationships, missed milestones, and a distance from loved ones that no professional achievement could fully close.

Leo knew he'd created something important. But he also knew there was a cost that could never be reversed.

### Reflection Question

How do you reconcile sacrifices for the greater good with their impact on your family?

# STORY 99 The Student's Year Off

Luna had the acceptance letter in hand, the dorm assignment ready, and the congratulatory posts from family queued up. But instead of packing for orientation, she bought a one-way ticket overseas.

While her classmates settled into lecture halls, Luna was navigating crowded train stations in languages she barely spoke, teaching English in rural schools, and learning how to make meals from scratch with host families who welcomed her like their own. She spent hours journaling in cafés, hiking remote trails, and asking strangers about their lives.

It wasn't all cinematic sunsets. When her friends posted photos in graduation gowns, she felt the sharp sting of comparison. She questioned if she'd traded too much— steady progress toward a degree for the uncertainty of a year spent wandering.

The *trade-off* was clear. She put off the safety and structure of the "next step" to follow a less predictable map.

The *benefit* was harder to measure but more enduring—resilience, adaptability, and a perspective that made the world feel both bigger and smaller at once.

The *consequence* was starting her career later than planned, carrying moments of doubt, and having to explain her resolve more times than she cared to.

When she finally stepped onto campus a year later, she didn't just know what she wanted to study—she knew *why* she wanted to study it. And she walked in not just as a student, but as someone ready to lead.

**Reflection Question**

How do you decide when to pause for self-discovery versus following the expected path?

# The Hand They Didn't Hold

Mike and Laura had always been "hands-on" parents. When their daughter Zoe faced challenges, they were quick to step in for teacher meetings, late-night editing of essays, and forgotten lunches delivered like clockwork.

But things changed when Zoe went to college, just a two-hour drive away. During her first semester, she called often: overwhelmed by classes, homesick, unsure if she belonged. Each time, Laura instinctively reached for her keys. Mike started researching nearby apartments.

But something made them pause.

They realized this was the threshold they'd been preparing her for her whole life. This wasn't just her chance to learn chemistry or literature. It was her chance to learn about *herself*.

So instead of swooping in, they listened. Encouraged. Let the silence stretch.

They stayed home.

The *trade-off* wasn't proximity; it was the comfort of rescuing, the illusion of control, the assurance that she wouldn't fall.

The *benefit* was watching Zoe rise, clumsily, haltingly, but on her own terms.

The *consequence* was hearing her struggle and not solving it. Letting go not of closeness, but of dependency.

And when she called months later to say, "*I figured it out. I'm doing okay now*," they cried, not out of sadness, but pride.

### Reflection Question

When do you show love not by stepping in—but by standing back and letting someone grow through the struggle?

# The Deadline
# He Let Pass

Hugo was a high-level executive at a leading tech firm, known for delivering results and outpacing deadlines. For years, he climbed the corporate ladder by saying yes to late meetings, red-eye flights, and calls that bled into weekends. Promotions came quickly. So did missed birthdays, empty chairs at school events, and peaceful dinners where he was mentally elsewhere.

Then one evening, as he was working on a presentation for a critical investor pitch, his phone buzzed.

It was a message from his wife: "*Emma just won her school's writing contest. I want you to be here when we surprise her with a cake.*"

The pitch was due by midnight. The team was waiting on him. Every instinct said: *Stay. Finish. Deliver.*

Instead, Hugo asked a cohort to take over, and he closed his laptop.

The *trade-off* was immediate. He missed out on delivering the pitch and getting the accolades.

The *benefit* was returning home to wide eyes, frosting-covered smiles, and the deep sense that, for once, he showed up where it mattered most.

The *consequence* was he was passed over for a lead on the next high-profile project. Another colleague stepped into the spotlight he'd been chasing.

But in choosing to be fully present that night, Hugo began rewriting his definition of success. It was less about constant advancement, more about being remembered in the rooms that didn't have corner offices.

### Reflection Questions

When success asks for more than you're willing to give, how do you decide what's truly worth sacrificing?

# PART III

# Reflection Guideposts

## Conclusion

# Reflect And Embrace

L ife often requires us to make sacrifices, sometimes without warning. At the end of the day, life is largely about choices—they often determine our happiness or our misery.

A few years after my dad passed away, while I was working on a presentation, my adult son, Matthew, who was visiting, asked me, "Why are you working at 7 a.m. on a weekend? The Formula 1 race in Monaco is about to begin." I applied the Sacrifice Framework, and I landed in the upper right quadrant. I should make the sacrifice. I chose to close the laptop, make some bacon and eggs, and watch the race with him, understanding that these moments matter.

As you finish this book, I urge you to reflect on your own sacrifices. Embrace them not with a sense of loss, but with the knowledge that they are stepping stones to a life well-lived, a life filled with purpose, connection, and fulfillment.

I want to challenge you: Take an inventory of your sacrifices. Ask yourself the following:

- What am I already giving up without realizing it?
- Are these the right things to sacrifice?
- What should I intentionally let go of to create space for what truly matters?

> Because here's the truth:
> Every success story isn't just built on what was gained, but on what was given up along the way.
> The question is—
> are you sacrificing the right things?

Your success, your happiness, will not be defined by how much you add to your life, but by how strategically you subtract.

It will be the sacrifices you made that were *worth it*. So, choose wisely. Choose meaningfully. Choose sacrifices that give your life purpose, connection, and fulfillment.

# Summary Of Categorized Reflection Questions

Use these guideposts as a quick map through the trade-offs in Part II. Each theme distills the heartbeat of the reflection questions and points you to the exact stories that probe that tension. If you're short on time, pick the theme that's pressing on you *right now*—then read those stories together and journal on the prompts.

## Family & Relationships

When love, loyalty, and presence collide with everything else: careers, goals, comfort, and timing. These questions press on how you protect the people who matter, without losing yourself.

**Referenced stories:** 3, 8, 14, 22, 27, 28, 31, 32, 33, 34, 41, 42, 43, 46, 49, 50, 53, 56, 58, 60, 61, 62, 64, 68, 75, 83, 91, 97, 100

## Career & Leadership

Ambition, authority, and the cost of moving up or stepping aside. These reflections ask what "success" is worth and how you lead when trade-offs are real humans.
**Referenced stories:** 11, 15, 70, 72, 80, 82

## Community & Service / Greater Good

Serving something bigger, such as students, neighbors, teammates, or a town. The questions here test how far you'll stretch for the common good, and when "yes" becomes too costly.
**Referenced stories:** 4, 10, 18, 21, 29, 36, 47, 48, 51, 55, 57, 59, 63, 69, 71, 73, 76, 79, 81, 87, 88, 89, 93

## Learning, Education & Early Choices

Grades, degrees, and the early forks in the road that ripple for years. These prompts explore when to chase the long view and what you're willing to miss right now to get there.
**Referenced stories:** 1, 9, 12, 35, 77

## Innovation & Entrepreneurship

Building the new: ideas, products, or companies. This theme wrestles with focus, risk, obsession, and what you're ready to trade for a shot at making something that lasts.
**Referenced stories:** 2, 17, 25, 26, 54, 86, 98

## Creativity & Calling

Art, craft, and the work only you can do. These questions probe integrity, solitude, and whether recognition is worth the price of admission.

**Referenced stories:** 7, 13, 16, 45, 67, 94

## Health, Energy & Boundaries

The fuel that makes everything else possible. These reflections force clarity on rest, limits, burnout, and the moment a noble push turns into self-erasure.

**Referenced stories:** 6, 19, 23, 30, 101

## Ethics & Integrity

Lines you won't cross, even when the payoff is shiny. These questions ask how your values cash out when real stakes are on the table.

**Referenced stories:** 37, 40, 52, 84

## Money & Security

Budgets, pay cuts, and living below your means on purpose. These prompts test when financial stability serves the mission and when it steals it.

**Referenced stories:** 65

## Place, Migration & Adventure

Moving, uprooting, and the pull of elsewhere, sometimes by choice, sometimes by necessity. These reflections weigh stability against the growth that only comes from going.

**Referenced stories:** 20, 24, 38, 74, 95, 96

## Resilience & Risk

Setbacks, near-misses, and the courage to reframe "failure" as tuition. These questions ask what you learned and how that learning will pay forward.

**Referenced stories:** 5, 78, 90

## Self-Discovery & Adventure

Sabbaticals, gap years, and the long look inward. These prompts explore pausing the conveyor belt to become someone you actually respect.

**Referenced stories:** 92, 99

*Tip:* Reading in clusters amplifies insight. For example, if you're debating a promotion that collides with family rhythms, pair Career & Leadership (11, 70, 72, 80, 82) with Family & Relationships (28, 31, 46. . .), and add a dose of Health, Energy & Boundaries (6, 15, 101). You'll feel the contours of your real trade-off fast.

# Appendix A
# Acknowledgments

I am deeply grateful to my family, friends, and colleagues who have supported me throughout this six-year journey. Your encouragement, patience, and belief meant more than you know.

To my wife, Jennifer, thank you for your unwavering support, especially during those late-night and last-minute writing sprints. Your patience, love, and understanding have been a key force that kept me going when the finish line felt far away.

To my team at Proactive Worldwide, especially Kelley Loiacono and Nando Scola. Your enthusiasm for this project, your thoughtful feedback, and your constant encouragement fueled my determination to see it through. You reminded me that this book isn't just about ideas, it's about people, relationships, and impact.

To my parents, who made countless sacrifices for me, my brothers, and others in their life, and showed us what it means to give up the right things to achieve what mattered most to them.

Over the past thirty-five years, my travels to over thirty countries have allowed me to meet remarkable individuals—clients, partners, mentors, strangers, and friends—whose stories, perspectives, and shared experiences have shaped how I view the world. Many of the insights in these pages were sparked by conversations in airports, conference rooms, and over late dinners in cities far from home. You've all contributed, whether you know it or not.

A special thanks to my publisher and editor, Henry DeVries, who believed early on that this topic was "a whale of an idea" that touches every human life. Your insights, honesty, and steady encouragement have been invaluable in bringing this book to life.

Finally, to everyone who has shared their own stories of sacrifice and resilience with me. You've made this book richer, more real, and more human.

## Appendix B
# About The Author

D avid Kalinowski is president and co-founder of Proactive Worldwide, Inc., a leading strategic intelligence consultancy established in 1995. With more than thirty-five years of Competitive Intelligence (CI) experience, David has led the firm in delivering over 7,500 global research and consulting engagements for 225+ Fortune 1000 companies. Under his leadership, Proactive has become a trusted partner for CI research, analysis, training, and consulting across a wide range of industries.

A dedicated educator and mentor, David has trained more than 3,000 CI professionals in over twenty-five countries. He is also deeply committed to giving back, actively volunteering and supporting philanthropic organizations, including the American Cancer Society, American Red Cross, Feed My Starving Children, National Fallen Firefighters Foundation, NIU Foundation, Purple Hearts, St. Jude's

Children's Research Hospital, Salvation Army, and Special Olympics.

David is the co-author of two bestselling books—*New Directions: A Competitive Intelligence Tale* (2011) and *The CI-Driven CEO* (2022).

He earned a B.S. in political science and public law from Northern Illinois University and has completed executive education programs at institutions such as MIT.

# Appendix C
# A Note From The Author

This book began to take shape in early 2019, as I approached the twenty-five-year mark of running the business I cofounded. After decades of business travel, missed family dinners, relentless deadlines, and personal trade-offs, I started asking myself questions I had long avoided: *Were all these sacrifices worth it? What did they cost? And what did they give me in return?*

I started asking others too—people I met on planes, in hotel lobbies, on client calls: "What's the biggest sacrifice you've ever made—and did it pay off?"

The answers were raw, personal, and profoundly human. Some sacrifices led to great rewards. Others ended in regret. But again and again, I noticed something: *most sacrifices are made in the moment, based on short-term emotions, without much thought about the long-term consequences or benefits.*

That tension fascinated me. It prompted me to dig deeper into the nature of sacrifice—what we give up, why we do it, and how we live with the outcomes.

*The Sacrifice Paradox* isn't a textbook. It's a reflection of the trade-offs I've wrestled with as a father, husband, son, business owner, friend, and flawed human being. It's built on stories—my own and those I've witnessed—that reveal how our most defining moments often come wrapped in discomfort and decisions we didn't want to make.

This isn't a book about suffering. It's a book about meaning. It's about how sacrifice, when done with purpose, doesn't deplete us; it refines us.

It's about that blurry line between ambition and presence.

It's about missing a deadline so you can make a memory.

It's about choosing family over comfort, truth over popularity, and sometimes, still getting it wrong.

If you've ever asked yourself, "*Was it worth it?*" then this book is for you.

Thank you for trusting me to get you thinking differently about the sacrifices you make.

I hope it meets you where you are—and leaves you changed.

With gratitude,
**David Kalinowski**

# Works Cited And
# Author's Notes

1   Stephen R. Covey, *The 8th Habit: From Effectiveness to Greatness* (Simon & Schuster, 2004), 79.

2   Michael E. Porter, "What is Strategy?" Harvard Business Review. November–December 1996

3   Suzy Welch, *10-10-10: A Life-Transforming Idea.* (Scribner, 2009).

4   Matthew Kelly, *The Rhythm of Life: Living Every Day with Passion & Purpose* (Touchstone, 2004).

5   Simon Sinek, *Find Your Why: A Practical Guide for Discovering Purpose for You and Your Team* (Portfolio, 2017), and his "Leading a Fulfilling Life" talks.

www.ingramcontent.com/pod-product-compliance
Lightning Source LLC
Chambersburg PA
CBHW031840200326
41597CB00012B/215